No High Adobe

High Adobe

DOROTHY L. PILLSBURY

Vignettes by
M. J. Davis

THE LIGHTNING TREE
JENE LYON, PUBLISHER
SANTA FÉ, NEW MEXICO   U.S.A.

BY DOROTHY L. PILLSBURY

No High Adobe

Adobe Doorways

Roots In Adobe

Star Over Adobe

NO HIGH ADOBE, Copyright © 1950, 1971 by The University of New Mexico Press. All rights reserved. Reprinted by special arrangement with The University of New Mexico Press.

Library of Congress Catalog Card No. 50-10958

ISBN: 0-89016-069-4 (PA)   ISBN: 0-89016-075-9 (CL)

MANUFACTURED IN THE UNITED STATES OF AMERICA

First Lightning Tree Edition—1983

THE LIGHTNING TREE   *Jene Lyon, Publisher*
P.O. Box 1837   Santa Fé, New Mexico 87504-1837   U.S.A.

Table of Contents

My Rich Neighbors

STRANGERS in Santa Fé look at the little adobe houses of the Apodacas and the Archuletas scattered at random over the landscape and exclaim, "How picturesque, how quaint." Then they add in troubled accents, "But the people must be terribly poor. It must be depressing. Why in the world did you buy a place in such a neighborhood?"

In spite of low money incomes, poverty is something I can never associate with my Spanish-American neighbors. Many of them own their own adobe homes and those homes possess a beauty for which rich Anglos strive in vain with the help of architects and decorators. They are indigenous—the product of centuries of living.

Sun pours in through deep-set windows. Rain purrs gently on flat roofs. The good adobe *tierra* produces, impartially, corn and yellow marigolds. There is room for a woman's pigment-hung clothesline and for a child's gambols. There is quiet for an old man's deep thought and the chatter of the piñon jay.

My neighbors are rich in time, that almost unrealized Anglo commodity. They go about their lives at an unhurried pace. There is time for simple courtesy, for flower tending, and for baby admiring.

They have an innate love of color and beauty. I find Mrs. Apodaca, her apron under her arm after a day's scrubbing in an Anglo kitchen, standing in the middle of the road where she can see the sunset-daubed mountains to the west. As the colors turn from rose to blue to deepest mulberry, she says, "Pretty tonight."

As I stumble through unlighted Tenorio Flat on a snowy night, I collide with old Timoteo Gurulé. *"Es bonita la nieve*—the snow is pretty," he remarks, unperturbed at the collision. A salmon-colored geranium blooming in an old lard can, a flight of bluebirds, a red and yellow apron, a kitten, a baby, *"es bonito"* if one is old and Spanish-speaking or "it is pretty" if one is young and English-speaking. Over and over the words echo through Tenorio Flat: *"es bonito*. It is pretty."

"Gracias" is another word that echoes around the little mud houses. When I ask Mrs. Apodaca how her family is, she replies, "All are well, *gracias."* And then she adds without self-consciousness, *"Gracias a Dios.* Thanks be to God."

"Hello, Manuelito," I call to the youngest toddler in the Flat. "How are you?" He is so young that I expect no reply. But he gives me the flicker of long, black eyelashes and answers sedately, "Fine, *gracias;* and you-oo-oo?"

My neighbors have an unaffected dignity. I meet Mrs. Apodaca as she starts out for a day's washing and scrubbing. *"Sí,"* says Mrs. Apodaca, "I help Mrs. Smeeth house-clean four days this week. Mrs. Smeeth is so busy with her clubs and her company and her hours and hours under the hair-drier."

Then Mrs. Apodaca breaks down and tells me the truth. "Maybe you have seen them, Señora, the sweaters in the store window down town. Red ones and purple ones and blue and yellow! One for Carmencita and one for Dado and one for Lupe and one for Luz. Four dollars each they cost. Mrs. Smeeth will pay me four dollars a day. I work four days."

Mrs. Apodaca walks serenely toward her cleaning job. If she were going out to take the Governor's dictation there could be no greater pride in her beshawled back. And I know, with inward chuckles, that she will work four days and four days only, no matter how much company "Mrs. Smeeth" may have nor how long she may have to sit under the hair-drier. Sixteen dollars will cover the expenditure Mrs. Apodaca has in mind. It would never enter her mind to work five days and have four dollars more than she needed for sweaters. She carries no umbrella for the Anglos' rainy day.

My neighbors are generous. When delicious odors seep out of the little adobe houses, I know it is only a matter of minutes until a little girl will appear at my door. *"Mamacita* thought you might like some little fried pies or some cheese-stuffed chiles or some blue-corn *tortillas.* She *wants* you to have them."

If a married son decides to bring his wife and family to the paternal home, adobe bricks soon add another room to the little mud house. There is always a corner for some homeless "old

4

one" by the big, black, wood-burning cook-stove. There is always indulgent affection for some motherless baby, and little blue shoes and pink silk bonnets to prove it.

My own home really begins in Tenorio Flat. Far down the dirt road I can smell the fragrance of their piñon fires. Their lamp-lighted windows guide me through the dark. Silhouetted against the snowy window stands Mrs. Apodaca, fussing with one of her geranium plants. Geraniums, sunsets, orange- and cherry-colored sweaters, piñon wood, and blue-corn *tortillas* she classifies simply as *dones de Dios*—gifts of God.

No High Adobe Wall

LIVING in such a neighborhood, all my Anglo friends thought I should have a high adobe wall around my long, narrow wedge of New Mexican soil. Everyone else did.

"You won't have any privacy without a wall," they warned. "Everyone who lives up on the hill or down on the flat has been using your lot for years as a short cut. They wander back and forth as if they owned it. Little boys will steal your fruit and little girls will walk off with your flowers. Oh, you'd better have a wall."

As I watched old ladies swathed in black shawls walking serenely through my premises, I clung to the whimsical thought that people might decorate my adobe soil even better than peaches ripening on ruffle-leaved trees or hollyhocks reaching for the housetop.

So it is that, after many years, my yard has become a thoroughfare and a neighborhood crossroads. Spanish-American children skim by like so many tropical birds. Their pink, yellow, and bright blue dresses outrival the best of my flowers. Nearly every small brown hand carries some kind of posey. I need no calendar to remind me of the progress of the seasons. They pass the windows of the Little Adobe House in the hands of school children—pussy willows and wild roses and golden aspen leaves and piñon branches starred with snow.

Two of the older girls finally plucked up courage to come in. One was Mrs. Apodaca's Carmencita and the other was a cousin who had the same name. They introduced themselves as Carmencita y Carmencita. As I was ironing they settled themselves comfortably on the couch. Would I like them to sing while I worked?

There was much whispering as the repertoire was planned. The little, short Carmencita "made" the alto and the tall, slim Carmencita "made" the soprano. Not everyone can finish an ironing to the cadences of the "Marines' Song" rolling out in Spanish or "America the Beautiful" sung by little girls whose ancestors were rooted in this adobe soil a full century before mine left the shores of England.

One winter night, working late at my desk by the corner fireplace, I had the feeling that someone was looking in the uncurtained window. I walked over and peered through the blossoming geranium plants. There, pressed against the glass, was a thatch of uncombed black hair dusted with snow, and two fascinated big brown eyes in a young face. "What do you want," I asked, opening the door.

"*Nada, nada*—nothing." And there was the sound of a half-swallowed sob. "I was only looking. It's so pretty—the fire and the cat and the flowers."

"Come in and look more," I invited. His name was Tomasito and he "had" twelve years. He was a *primo*—a cousin of Mrs. Apodaca. His father's name was Canuto and he was mad at him. That was why he had left home. With the Spanish love of the dramatic, he added, "Tomorrow I go see if they take me in the Air Corps."

In the middle of the night, Tomasito and I made hot chocolate, Mexican style with a dash of cinnamon. He drank three cups and consumed a half-dozen sandwiches. Then, in front of the chuckling piñon fire, we listened to all my records of Spanish music. When that was finished Tomasito had decided to postpone his aviation career and to return to the adobe of *"el papá."*

On summer evenings I like to see old ladies in long, full-gathered black skirts and old men in their wide-brimmed, black felt hats wandering decorously through my yard. Mr. Apodaca's early morning *"Buenos días"* starts my day with zest. When night wraps the Little Adobe House in blue and purple shadows, I catch Mrs. Apodaca's soft-spoken, *"Vaya con Dios—*Go with God," as she slips like another shadow past the candle-lighted window.

I glory in other people's adobe walls when snow lies along their tops, or when apple blossoms tap along their sides, or when the Carmencitas and Manuelitos sit on their topmost bricks and sing on moonlight summer nights. But I will have no walls, however charming, around my wedge of adobe soil. After all, what is privacy? Compared to the pageantry that passes through my yard, it might be a kind of vacuum.

The Odyssey of Mrs. Apodaca

SOMETHING momentous was happening in Tenorio Flat. Women left their clotheslines half filled with pink and yellow dresses and gathered together in low-voiced groups. After work, men in broad-brimmed, black felt hats entered Mrs. Apodaca's adobe and, after a time, came out talking seriously. Even the *muchachos* stopped their play and peered curiously in between the geranium plants on the window sill.

After many days of continued conferences, Armendita Apodaca brought a much creased letter to the Little Adobe House. Sternly I squelched my surging curiosity and talked politely of unimportant matters. At last she said: "My brother, Miguelito, has been living a long time in California. He has two little boys *mamacita* has never seen."

"Yes, yes," I nodded.

"And there are a lot of *primos*—cousins."

Again I nodded, hoping not to break the thread of unraveling mystery.

"So Miguelito and the *primos* have written a letter. They want *mamacita* to come to Los Angeles to see them. They even sent a money-order, enough for her train fare and everything."

"Wonderful!" I exclaimed. "How happy your mother must be. When is she leaving?"

Armendita shrugged her shoulders and wrinkled her smooth forehead. "I don't know. She can't make up her mind. Some of the neighbors say 'go' and some say 'don't go.' We have all talked and talked."

So that was the reason for all the conferences —as big a problem in their little adobe world as peace plans in capitals!

"I thought," Armendita continued, "that as you have been in California, maybe you could encourage *mamacita* if I brought her over. She is scared to go so far. But Miguelito and the *primos* will be sad if she doesn't come to see them. And all that money they've saved!"

In a few moments she came, dragging a balking *mamacita*. I described, in my best words, Hollywood, where the *"cines"* were made, and Los Angeles with its big Spanish-American population. I painted word pictures of miles of flowers—roses climbing over the very roof tops, palms growing by the roadsides, and geraniums as tall as adobe walls.

I think it was the geraniums that steeled Mrs. Apodaca to attempt the great adventure. She had never been on a train. In all her life she had never been out of Santa Fé but to return to the Spanish-American villages tucked away in New Mexico's mountain fastnesses.

Minor difficulties called for further neighborhood conferences. Should she or should she not take the two younger Apodacas with her? This idea being vetoed promptly, we turned our efforts to the question of suitable apparel for the traveler. Mrs. Apodaca absolutely refused to discard her long, full-gathered black skirts, her decent, black cotton stockings, and the enveloping shawl about her head.

"If the movie directors ever see you in that outfit," I warned, "they'll grab you off the street and put you in a picture. And then you'll never get back to Santa Fé."

Mrs. Apodaca giggled at the idea, but it evidently had some weight. Shortly I was invited to the dress rehearsal of her new traveling clothes. She kept pulling frantically at the skirt of her new blue dress. She had let the hem out until it came half way to her ankles, but I could see she considered it a scandal. A little flat hat, like a kettle-lid was pinned precariously to the coil of her blue-black hair. She kept grabbing at it as if a gale were blowing through the quiet of her snug, thick-walled rooms.

Tenorio Flat settled down after Mrs. Apodaca's departure. I smiled every time I thought of her arrival in Los Angeles' fine railway station. She had taken with her a battered old suitcase, tied together with rope, and four gay wicker baskets. All her baggage emitted a beguiling odor of little fried pies stuffed with piñon nuts, rounds of homemade goat cheese and hand-pounded chile paste.

What was my horror, on the tenth day, to see a well-known figure, its head bound with a flour sack, drawing water from the blue-covered well.

"*Sí,* Miguelito and the *primos* were fine. *Sí,* Los Anhelees was fine. *Sí,* the geraniums were beeg. *Sí,* it was *bueno* to be home." She was start-

13

ing spring house-cleaning and was going to whitewash that very day.

That was all I could find out about the momentous journey until Armendita came over with another letter. "Miguelito says," Armendita groaned, "*mamacita* disappeared every morning after he went to work and didn't get back until night. She went to a place called Olvera Street and stayed there all day."

"Olvera Street," I chuckled, "is a street Los Angeles has kept Spanish. There are little wayside booths and stoves where you can buy *frijoles* and *tortillas*."

"She never saw the ocean. She never saw the *cine*. She didn't eat in a big cafeteria," wailed Armendita.

"Never mind," I comforted. "You'd be surprised how many world travelers do just the same thing."

New Mexican Wood Smoke

MRS. APODACA and I have corner fireplaces, where we burn vast quantities of piñon wood. When the cottonwoods begin to drop their leaves, Mr. Apodaca deserts his job for a week, borrows a *primo's* truck, departs for the mountains, and brings in the winter's supply. So do all the other men of Tenorio Flat. Soon Santa Fé takes on its distinctive aura of piney fragrance. It comes spiraling out of hundreds of squat little chimneys. It drifts about sunny *placitas* and snarls all the little adobe houses in a net of comfort and well-being.

Things are not so easy for me. I call Mrs. Archuleta, whose husband owns a small local woodyard. Although there is a Mr. Archuleta, his wife always answers, "Mrs. Pomposo Archuleta's woodyard." That is, if she answers the phone.

Usually it is one of the younger Archuletas who answers my call.

"*Qué?*" asks a thin, bashful, downhill voice.

"*Su mamá,*" I request.

"*Mamá, mamá.*" There is a shrill hubbub of children's voices. *Mamá* is evidently far afield—perhaps drawing water from the well with the bright, blue cover or feeding the goats in a far corner of the yard. A little breathless, she retrieves the *teléfono.*

"I need piñon wood, Mrs. Archuleta. Winter has sneaked up on us again. Such a wind down Canyon Road! There'll be snow before morning."

Calmly Mrs. Archuleta ignores the ferocity of the elements. If a blizzard were snarling over our defenseless mesaland, she would observe the amenities in proper sequence.

"*Cómo está?*" she inquires in her most concerned conversational tone.

"I am well, *gracias,*" I admit, hurriedly taking my rightful place in the ceremony. "But a little chilly, due to no piñon wood. You know the way I like it—not over twelve inches long and—"

"And *su mamá?*" persists Mrs. Archuleta, with a slight note of reproof.

16

"My mother is well, *gracias*, but her feet are cold, due to no piñon wood for the—"

"And *su gato*, Koshare?" continues Mrs. Archuleta with much sweetness, but firmness.

"My cat, Koshare, is in the best of health, *gracias*, but is unhappy because the little *fogón* [fireplace] has no warmth."

That being the extent of my family, it is now my turn to make the polite inquiries. "And how are you and *su esposo* [your husband]? And *los muchachos*—Margarita, Josefa, Vincente, Sabina, and Solomón—are they all enjoying good health?"

"*Todos*—all—Señora, *gracias a Dios.*"

Then, and only then, am I permitted to return to the mundane subject of firewood and my cold hearth-stone. "*Sí, sí*, they will bring the piñon wood just as I like it—short but of a fatness."

From long experience I know it is useless, but I suggest: "Could you—could you deliver it tomorrow?"

Mrs. Archuleta is shocked by such unseemly haste, but she will not betray her outraged feelings by giving me a point blank refusal. "I couldn't promise it tomorrow."

"The next day, Tuesday then?"

"I couldn't promise it Tuesday."
I mention in turn every day of the week.
At last I come to Saturday. That is five days off.
"*Sí, sí, sábado.* I can promise it for *sábado.*"
I sigh with relief. As I am about to hang up,
Mrs. Archuleta breaks in with an afterthought.
"I almost forgot, Señora, do you want a one-
burro load or a two-burro load?"

"A four-burro load," I order recklessly. The
wood will be delivered in a rickety truck smelling
of gasoline, but Mrs. Archuleta clings to the old
measurements as she clings to the old courtesies.

It wasn't so long ago that all the wood used
in Santa Fé's hundreds of fireplaces came down
from the mountains on burroback. The wood-
gatherer drove his string of *burritos* from door to
door. All through the golden autumn days, the
high-walled streets of Santa Fé were crowded
with burros so laden with wood that they looked
like wood piles that had miraculously sprouted
fuzzy ears and delicate little feet. When summer
came, the little animals were turned loose upon
the town. They brayed dolefully by the light of
the moon from amid cherished flower beds. They
foraged undeterred on the lawn of the Governor.
They were a community institution.

Open fireplaces, blazing piñon logs, and the scent of wood smoke are as much a part of Santa Fé as the piñon-freckled hills and cloud-shadowed mountains that hold the old town in their great, warm, hollow hand. The whitewashed corner *fogón* is such a small, simple object to give so much comfort. No andirons are used. The logs are stood on end, leaning against one another. They give the effect of an outdoor campfire, moved into a corner of the home. Sometimes you glance up hurriedly in the evening shadows to see if a chipmunk is not scurrying along the pine tree ceiling beams. You almost expect to see a spotted fawn emerge from a darkened angle by the bookcase.

Little
Piñon Fires

A BLUE CANDLE
was burning before the uncurtained window of
the Little Adobe House. Another candle, on the
shelf of the corner fireplace, coaxed piñon flames
to higher soarings. Whitewashed walls blushed
Christmas red in the dim room.

Suddenly Carmencita Apodaca's many-
curled head appeared like a ghost outside the
square-paned window. Before I could open the
door, she was gone. But in a few minutes, there
was her mother's shawl-wrapped figure tapping
to come in. A plate of little fried pies, bursting
with piñon nuts, was in her hand.

"I say to Carmencita," Mrs. Apodaca explained, "run see if the Señora has her lamp
lighted. If she has, she is working and I will not
molest her. But, if the blue candles burn, the
Señora will be sitting by her fire doing nothing."

Mrs. Apodaca settled herself in the big rocker and pushed her best shawl back on her shoulders. From her ears dangled half circles of soft old gold and on her brown index finger a big turquoise in a hand-wrought, silver setting gesticulated with elegance.

"The *muchacha* say," Mrs. Apodaca covered her smile politely with a brown hand, " 'the Señora does *nada, nada*.' "

"I was thinking," I replied, slightly on the defensive. "Nothing like a piñon fire for thoughts that sing."

"*Sí*," nodded Mrs. Apodaca in complete understanding, "but it is strange that, being an Anglo lady, you can do it. Busy, busy, the Anglo ladies, the club, the PTA, the *teléfono,* the hairdrier, the book-of-the-month."

"I was thinking about Christmas here in Santa Fé," I explained, "simple and gay for the eyes and tender and warm for the heart, like our burning piñon pyres along the crooked snowy streets."

"*Sí, es bueno,*" Mrs. Apodaca agreed, not overly impressed.

"Maybe it's because we are seven thousand feet nearer the stars than many other places," I elaborated. "Maybe it's because I know shepherds are watching their flocks in sheltered valleys. And little picture-book Spanish-American villages still keep ancient mellow ways."

Suddenly Mrs. Apodaca was thinking with me. Her big brown eyes were shining, her golden earrings danced, and the silver setting of her big ring focused a ray of firelight.

"Ah, Señora, the little villages! When a *muchacha*, I lived in one over by Truchas Peak. Cedar forests in the deep cañons! And snow burying the little houses! Goats' bells tinkling all night long. No one from outside came near us. Such processions around the windy plaza, where the piñon pyres lighted the whole place on *Nochebuena*. I can hear the fiddles and guitars even now, and the old Spanish songs.

"Once, Señora, I wore a blue cape and rode all over the village on a *burrito*. The wind blew my window-curtain veil straight out behind and I had to hold my tinsel crown on with both hands. Desiderio Dominguez (you have heard of him, Señora. He is a *político* now) had a carpenter's box tied on his skinny *muchacho* shoulders. With all the village following us, we went from door to door asking lodging for the night.

"And once, you may not believe it, Señora, I played in the old play where Good and Evil battle and Good always wins. My *mamacita* taught me the words as her *mamacita* had taught her." Words in the old plays came down in families, like earrings of gold.

"And even in Santa Fé," continued Mrs. Apodaca, "there are many of the old ways left. No? I was sad, only a few years ago when the procession of the wood-haulers stopped. In those days all of the wood for Santa Fé came down from the mountains on burroback. Ah, being a wood-hauler was an honorable calling! Late on the afternoon before Christmas, the wood-haulers, in their best jackets and *pantalones,* and the *burritos,* brushed until their coats were as soft as kittens' fur, made a procession. Around the plaza they marched and all Santa Fé out in the dusk of *Nochebuena* to see them. And then a big piñon fire would be lighted in front of the cathedral. At that signal all the crooked, narrow streets would burst out with the flame from hundreds of other little piñon fires along the way."

Mrs. Apodaca slapped her shawl about her head. "Too long I molest you with my words. I go now to save the *muchachos* from a sea of tissue paper. They are wrapping gifts from the Five and Dime. No gifts in my day, Señora, not until Twelfth Night. Then we left straw in our shoes outside the door, for the camels of the Three Kings. It was always gone in the morning and in its place were sweets."

As I opened the door, we both exclaimed, "The first little piñon fire!" There it was up against the black mountain, lighting the way to some story-book village. *"Es bueno,"* Mrs. Apodaca nodded, *"El Santo Niño* will find his way through the dark, bitter night."

Young Mr. Abeyta

WHEN SNOW covers the winding ways of Tenorio Flat, I find myself without the local paper. Delivery boys do not like to plow through the drifts for a single delivery. So I had resigned myself to a winter's deprivation of flavorsome local news. But suddenly a paper appeared in the be-mittened hand of a small boy.

"Mrs. Apodaca said I was to bring you a paper every day," he said, blinking snowflakes from long, black lashes. "Me, I deliver another part of town, but I live in Tenorio Flat. If you don't mind getting your paper late, I'll bring it over when I get home."

"Wonderful," I rejoiced. "And what is your name?"

"Just call me Mr. Abeyta," said the small one, with the flash of a smile like a beacon light.

All through the winter, as late as nine o'clock, Mr. Abeyta brought my paper with punctilious regularity. If away from home, I would find it tucked, neatly folded, behind the screen door. If at home, I enjoyed the boy more than the paper. Many times Mr. Abeyta came through wind, darkness, and deep snow with the paper shielded under his thin, shabby coat. Always he handed it to me as if this final job was the crowning event of a most exciting day.

Evidently his attitude was contagious, for soon a string of satellites accompanied Mr. Abeyta to my door. The job had taken on the nature of an expedition. On snowy nights, they had their legs bound with strips of burlap in lieu of boots. Mr. Abeyta led the way through the dark night, with a candle in an old tin coffee can. His followers were roped together with a length of clothesline, like mountain climbers. "Take it easy, men," Mr. Abeyta would call in his thin treble. "Look out for the *precipicio* under the plum tree."

When summer came and the regular boy took over his routine duties, I wondered to what new adventures Mr. Abeyta would turn his dramatic talents.

One day, following the old Indian Trail, where it crosses the river, I found Mr. Abeyta and his faithful followers engaged in a vast engineering project. They were damming the Río Santa Fé with boulders and fallen trees and constructing their own swimming-pool.

After that, I timed my visits to the plaza so that I might have sight of the intrepid engineers sauntering homeward in the late afternoon. Sleek and content they were, with blue-black heads still moist from their splashings. Somehow the scent of willows and splotched sunshine clung to them like an atmosphere. Their complete well-being was as warm and radiating as the comfort of sun-baked adobe walls.

Later, Mr. Abeyta achieved the seemingly unattainable for a boy who lived in a little mud house and whose father was a day laborer. Mr. Abeyta acquired a horse. He became a *caballero*. That horse was probably the most disreputable in all the state—evidently someone's discarded work horse. To see Mr. Abeyta, with the horse tied to a cottonwood tree, currying the hide that had once been a dubious white but which was now a dingy yellow, was to bring a catch to the heart. The animal's wide back swayed along the spine like a sagging adobe wall, and its huge feet were made for the hauling of squeaking *carretas*.

To Mr. Abeyta, that relic of a horse was a caparisoned charger. By dint of much toiling in Anglo gardens, he acquired a costume in keeping with his mount. New, bright-blue levis met handmade cowman's boots with high heels and an appliqued design of flowers and fruits in white leather around the tops. His shirt was apple green, set off at the throat by a kerchief of flaming, chile-red satin. Not for Mr. Abeyta was the battered ten-gallon hat of the region. Somewhere he had found a real *vaquero's* hat, flat of crown and wide of brim. It was held in place under his brown chin by two thongs of rawhide. It gave him a decidedly South American aspect.

To see Mr. Abeyta clumping down Garcia Street was to see Pegasus and the Rider to the Sun. One hand folded back negligently over his slim hip, his back was arrow straight. His eyes shone with a somewhat supercilious fire and his square, white teeth were a flash of light under the shadow of his *vaquero's* hat. He was a sensation all along the dirt road section.

Little girls dallied at road intersections to see Mr. Abeyta ride by. Anglo boys got off their fine, shining bicycles and stood wistfully gazing as the *caballero* passed. They did not seem to see the clumping, ancient horse. They saw Mr. Abeyta, horseman.

At *fiesta* time, in the procession of De Vargas and the *Conquistadores,* some of the finest horses of the state are paraded by elegantly costumed, silver-decked riders. Watching the thoroughbreds and slender-footed Arabians pass, what was my amazement to see a familiar sway-backed creature pounding along between an aristocratic black and an arch-necked Palomino.

I had to look twice to be sure, for Mr. Abeyta had risen to new dramatic heights. With a bit of charcoal he had contrived sideburns, a Spanish goatee, and curling mustachio on his brown face. It was certainly Mr. Abeyta right in the midst of *los Conquistadores.*

A Custom
of the Country

WHEN I ASK
Mrs. Apodaca stupid and sometimes impertinent
questions, she shrugs be-shawled shoulders, rolls
her eyes heavenward, and flutters small brown
hands. *"Es costumbre del país,"* she enunciates
with finality. "It is the custom of the country."

One disturbing custom of the country oc-
curs yearly, in midsummer when apricots dangle
golden globes against old walls and pears blow
themselves into elongated jade balloons. Past
the Little Adobe House, in chattering groups,
wander the *muchachos* of Tenorio Flat, each
openly carrying a salt or sugar sack.

Young Mr. Abeyta, jaunty in his *vaquero's*
hat, forsakes his ancient steed. He and his satellites wave gaily as they pass. Decorous little girls,
with the saintly expressions of medieval cherubs,
trot by on their nefarious way. Toddlers, sup-

porting one another's unsteady steps, struggle along in the rear.

And I know that, before nightfall, Anglos for miles around will be in the wildest excitement. They will be calling my little friends "young barbarians." The local police will hear high pitched, Anglo voices demanding arrest and punishment.

For all the Anglo trees will have been stripped of fruit as neatly as if a cloud of locusts had passed by. In a semi-desert land, where each golden apricot and each ruddy plum is the result of cherishing and prolonged care, such a loss is a major catastrophe. Not only is the fruit gone, but tender tree limbs are broken and flower beds are trampled and littered with half-eaten, green fruit.

Toward night, police cars appear in Tenorio Flat. Uniformed men, nearly all of Hispanic origin, talk with be-shawled *mamás,* of inscrutable expression. The police are lenient. Likely as not their own Manuelitos and María Tranquilas are involved. Likely as not they, themselves, remember the peculiar sweetness of stolen apricots on the tongue.

"*Sí, sí,* I will tell their *papá* when he comes

from his work at the Gas Company," Mrs. Apodaca reassures the representatives of law and order. But, at night, there is no evidence that the adobe equivalent of the Yankee woodshed is being used for disciplinary purposes. All is serene in Tenorio Flat.

Anglos do not know that fruit-stealing is a custom of the country and is not considered stealing at all. Mixed with the Spanish strain of many of my neighbors is a strong thread of the Indian. And the Indians believe that the fruits of the Earth-Mother belong to all her children. There is no mine and thine. It is said that warring Pueblos and Navahos wandered at will in each other's territory to pick, without strife, the harvest of piñon nuts produced by the forests.

I tried to remember this when, year after year, my own fruit trees were raided by the same *muchachos* who were otherwise so honest I could leave garden tools scattered about the yard and doors and windows of the Little Adobe House unlocked or open, whether I was there or not.

In an effort to circumvent the custom of the country, I hit upon a plan that seemed worth trying. Little did I dream that the custom of the country was a labyrinth in whose maze an Anglo might become hopelessly lost. "If you don't take the half-ripe fruit which isn't good for anything," I promised Mr. Abeyta, "I'll share all the fruit with you when it is ripe."

Not a peach was touched that year—not a fragrant plum, not a yellowing balloon of pear. On the appointed day of harvest, thirty *muchachos* stormed the quiet Little Adobe House. In despair, I turned the whole matter over to young Mr. Abeyta and retreated from a situation with which I could not cope. Young Mr. Abeyta was in his element. He, and he alone, climbed the trees and picked the fruit. Not one branch was broken. Then he asked for newspapers. There must be one for each *muchacho* and one for the Señora, "because she watered the trees."

As a crowning touch, they called for brooms and carefully swept up every fallen leaf, every pit, and every bit of skin. The yard was in much better condition than it had been before thirty children had swarmed over the adobe soil. I went about quite smug and contented over the way I had guided and directed the custom of the country. In my conceit and ignorance, I did not realize that I had but wandered into a maze of folk ways from which I could never extricate myself.

Before night, Mr. Abeyta and his satellites appeared with a big sack of the finest, most luscious apricots I had ever seen. "For you," said Mr. Abeyta, removing his *vaquero* hat with a flourish. "We *want* you to have them."

"Chimayó apricots," I gloated, knowing that Tenorio Flat had many relatives living in the sunny valley, famous for its fruit. They had shared with me the gift of some broad-hatted relative. Then I remembered another custom of the country. It is an Indian custom that a gift from a friend shall never go unrequited. Receiving and giving must flow in an endless current.

As I pondered these gentle thoughts, the telephone broke in on my serene meditations. "That gang of young barbarians from Tenorio Flat raided my apricot trees today," the voice shrilled. "I had to go down to the plaza for an hour. Not one apricot did they leave for me and I tended those trees like orchids. I've called the police."

My eyes strayed sadly to the little wicker basket that held the few remaining apricots I had not consumed in innocence and in illusion.

Mother of Seas

"WHEN I WAS in Los Anhelees," said Mrs. Apodaca, a note of regret in her voice, "I did not see the ocean. You, Señora, must miss that ocean very much in this high, dry country."

Oddly enough I have missed that endless expanse of blue water so little that it is only after many years that it seems important to find a reason why. The reason is that I still have a sea. It is overhead in the illimitable turquoise sky of New Mexico. A more tenuous, a more subtile, sea it is, but vastly more appealing because of its intangible qualities.

The New Mexican sky is like no other I have ever seen. It is not a stationary painted ceiling tacked solidly overhead. It is alive, ever moving, given to dramatic violence and gentle whimsy.

Cloud ships ply that overhead sea. Their white sails fill with all the winds as they skim on airy voyages. They pause briefly at ethereal ports of call behind the mulberry Jemez Mountains or the pink Sandias. Toward evening, most of them return to their home port, high over the wooded mountains of Santa Fé. At sunset, their mastheads shake out pennants and signal flags, whose code meanings I can only guess. Does the jade-green flag mean the discovery of some New World in the sky? Does the amethyst bunting celebrate rich cargoes of star dust and spices from the stratosphere?

Often in midsummer, I have started for the plaza with the sky sea as innocent and sun-filled as a mill pond. Within an hour, I have slunk home wet to the skin by a sudden downpour, my once crisp dress as limp as a wisp of fog and my hat collapsed about my ears.

The sea overhead gives no warning of its whimsical intent. Flat roofs hiss with the violent onslaught. Little wooden gutters spout like fire hoses. Mrs. Apodaca wraps her shawl about her and rushes out with her geranium plants from the blue painted window sill. Almost before *los muchachos* can be herded into the house, out comes the sun again in the most tranquil of skies.

Against the soft gauze of northern mountains, a rainbow bridge is constructed in the twinkling of an eye. One bastion is anchored to the purple mesa, near Glorieta, its opposite end is fastened to the big cottonwood tree that shades the old plaza at San Ildefonso. That is something my more material sea never had—soaring arches of jasper and tourmaline erected without workmen and without toil.

The overhead sea revels in dramatic exhibitions in winter. I have started for the hills in the most beguiling of sunlight. Irises were poking up their green, inquisitive noses. Willows showed a red springtime lacquer. Suddenly elfin laughter rippled overhead. A blizzard roared along the crooked streets of Santa Fé. The little adobe houses peered out amazed from a packing of lambs' wool.

Sometimes, at dawn and sunset, dream cities rear their battlements on sky islands. For the overhead sea has no shore line. That is its greatest charm. In spite of its immensity, it has moments when it sags close to earth as if it had a secret it wanted to whisper. Riding or trudging up steep, tawny hills, I indulge in a new sport which I call sky jumping. It is characteristic of high places in New Mexico that the summit seems to have no connection with the weary way up. One's inclination is to take off into blue space without a glance at the downward trail.

Companionship with the sea overhead grows richer with the years. Especially at night! Then the ethereal sea draws near with wind-fluted murmurings a human can understand. Gone are the day's dramatic displays. Gone are the hilarious junketings of adventurous cloud sails and lavish outpourings of color. At night the sky sea drops lower and lower over little adobe houses, as if it had a great concern for the inhabitants. Just to show that it is not a creation of prank and whimsy, it hangs decorous stars in the darkness. They shine like riding-lights on the masts of the cloud ships riding at anchor in the calm port of home.

The Valley
of Cousins

"UP IN THE
county of Río Arriba," said Mrs. Apodaca, rolling her eyes and gesticulating. From the light on
her face and the softness in her voice I gathered
that the county of Río Arriba was Mrs. Apodaca's
El Dorado of the heart. Nowhere in all New
Mexico did hollyhocks grow to such forest-like
heights as they did in the county of Río Arriba.
Nowhere were little adobe houses so golden and
so sun-soaked. Nowhere were people so kindly
and *simpático*.

All I knew of the county of Río Arriba was
that it was a sparsely-settled county close to the
Colorado line, where old Spanish-Colonial ways
live on serenely in an American state. All
through the spring months, my desire to see Mrs.
Apodaca's El Dorado increased with the flower-
ing of peach blossoms against brown adobe walls

and the lavender brush stroke of lilacs overflowing my boundary line.

The desire reached its climax early one June in wartime. I approached Mrs. Apodaca in desperation. "There must be some way for me to get to the county of Río Arriba."

"*Sí*," Mrs. Apodaca pursed thoughtful lips. "*Sí*, there is a bus, a very little bus, that crosses the county of Río Arriba. I took it once to visit my *prima*, who lives in Tierra Amarilla. She had twin babies, María Estefanita and María Eulalia. It was a terrible journey, Señora. The little bus has few springs. A hundred miles up to the Colorado line and a hundred miles back! The bus leaves Santa Fé at the first crow of the cock and does not return until in the night. Not even for María Estefanita and María Eulalia would I make such a trip again."

I found the little bus in the pearly light of early morning. The conveyance was all Mrs. Apodaca had described. It was not much larger than a touring car and was travel-scarred and mud-plastered. On its top was a rack, where the battered and rope-tied baggage of the passengers was to rattle around for a hundred miles.

Spanish flowed up and down the bus like a

sea. I was the only Anglo in its crowded interior. A girl in her teens shared the seat with me. On her lap was a large, straw, black-lacquered hat ornamented with a red and blue rose of great size and stiffness. She held the hat carefully and kept flicking away the dust that settled on its shining surface.

"I spend four days with my *madrina* [godmother] in Santa Fé," she confided. "I go to the *cine* every day and I buy a hat." She held the hat at arm's length and studied it happily. From a green oilcloth purse, she produced rows of stamp pictures. "And I have my picture taken. See, this one is with the hat on."

It was at Abiquiu that I first realized that I was in the Valley of the Cousins. Other little buses, as battered as our own, were pulling in with enticing names on them—Ojo Caliente, Antonito. I had to stifle a wild desire to forsake my destination to see what the other little towns were like. From every bus, brown arms and heads extended. Happy eyes beamed and delighted voices called, *"Ah, primo."* I wondered if everyone traveling in this far-flung country was related. *"Ah, primo! Comó está, primo?"*

As we bumped slowly along again, I did not wonder that the county of Río Arriba had assumed such spotlighted place in Mrs. Apodaca's thoughts. The landscape simply stood up and sang in a chorus of color. Arroyos gashed it—layer on layer of brilliant blue, rust, ocher, and green. Mesas bisected it with ruler-straight horizontal lines, drawn with colored crayons.

In the midsts of such thoughts, it was disconcerting to see my seat companion lean from the window to salute an old man sitting far back on the rump of a burro. *"Ah, primo!"* Or to greet a woman dragging her long full skirts along the dusty road edge. *"Ah, prima,* I return now from Santa Fé."

It seemed strange that a country formed on such gigantic lines and embroidered with fantasy, should hold such friendly, simple people. But in sheltered nooks I saw their mellow, walled homes, their blue-hooded wells, and heard the tinkle of goats' bells.

A river flows through the town on the Colorado border, where we finally halted for some hours. Up and down the streets, little ditches have been formed to carry water from melting snows to such flower gardens as I had never seen. Lemon lilies, delphinium, roses, stock grew in a brilliance of color that seemed derived from the highly colored landscape. Wherever I stopped, out would come the owner to heap my arms with cuttings, seeds, and bulbs until I looked like an advertisement for a seed catalogue by the time I got on the bus for the return trip.

That night, as I felt my way through the dark of Tenorio Flat, I saw Mrs. Apodaca's shadowy, shawl-draped figure between the geranium plants in her window. *"Gracias a Dios,"* she whispered. "You are safely home at last, Señora."

"Tell me," I asked, shoving seeds, seedlings, and bulbs through the window into her hands, "is everyone in the county of Río Arriba related? I never saw so many cousins in all my life."

"No," said Mrs. Apodaca, smiling gently at my ignorance, "not by blood, Señora. *Primo,* it is a word of the heart."

On the
Little Bird Plateau

SANTA FÉ
still remembers that early August day, several
years ago, when it was shaken to its adobe core.
Poplars and cottonwoods were languidly shaking
green feather dusters at the sky. Even the piñon
jay modulated his strident voice.

In the midst of its full summer calm, the
ancient city stirred suddenly. Almost within its
mellowed confines, the world-shattering atom
bomb had been evolved. Santa Fé could not believe it. It was totally out of character.

Step by step, the little old-world city
thought back to 1943. That was when the Los
Alamos School, an hour's drive away, above the
Pajarito Plateau, had been taken over by the
Government. Even to the boys' saddle horses, it
was said!

And then a harassed man with a big brief

case had appeared in the town's small employment office. "I want cooks," he demanded, "chief cooks, fry cooks, bull cooks, and waiters—thirty or forty of them. There's a lot of construction going on at Los Alamos. We have to feed the workers."

The employment office attendant had gasped. It had become increasingly difficult to produce one *rebozoed* grand-dame for house work. "Advertise," demanded the stranger. "Offer high wages. Here is what we will pay." The attendant gasped again. Never had such wages been offered in Santa Fé.

The next morning her small office was filled with a motley crowd who had evidently scraped adobe mud from brown fingers in response to unheard-of wages. In excited Spanish they insisted they could cook and wait table, in spite of the blue overalls and many-angled felt hats that marked them as adobe men, shepherds, and ranchers. The harassed gentleman hired every one of them. They disappeared up on the plateau.

Trucks, heavily laden, began to shake the narrow, crooked streets of Santa Fé. Householders complained that adobe walls were cracking and settling along the truck route. Smoke veiled the distant plateau. Sometimes at night there were dazzling fires against the sky.

At the time, Santa Fé had its own theories of what was happening in its back yard. Old Timoteo Gurulé stood half an hour in the snow, explaining his idea. "Ah, Señora," he held forth, "it is to train the men who walk on the little wooden runners up the snowy mountains and then spread their arms on the very tops and fly down the other side. I saw them once in the *cine*."

"Ski troops," I nodded.

"*¡Verdad!*" Timoteo beamed. "Plenty of mountains, Señora, the Jemez, the Taos, the Sandias, and our own. Without a doubt it is to train the *soldados* of the little wooden runners."

Gradually the words, Los Alamos, dropped from the vocabulary of Santa Fé. It was indicative of the discreet policy that prevailed that we now referred to the place as Up-On-The-Hill. People disappeared Up-On-The-Hill. A young scientist I had known elsewhere paused briefly in my adobe with his wife and child.

"Are you taking a vacation out here?" I asked, bewildered by their sudden appearance.

46

"No," said the scientist, "going to work here."

"But what is there in your profession?"

"Up-On-The-Hill," he explained without further comment.

Months later, I saw them again. They were wandering vaguely about the hotel lobby. We nodded and spoke as if we were the merest acquaintances. Up-On-The-Hill had become a kind of Lost World.

Often sitting by my corner fireplace on a winter night, I thought of the people in trucks and cars who turned off the highway, headed for their strange, isolated life on the Hill. Did they realize that by one of the most fantastic patterns of history, their secret modern project was taking place in surroundings so ancient the mind of man could only guess and surmise? Did they sometimes glance at Black Mesa and the sleepy plaza of San Ildefonso in its shadow? Did they wonder about the cliff dwellings of Frijoles?

When the news of what actually had taken place on the Hill broke over Santa Fé's quiet streets, I thought of the plateau where scholars had knelt in the dust to sift the colorful soil in the hope of finding some slight clue to the life of a great prehistoric people who had vanished from the earth. Almost grain by grain those scholars had endeavored to reconstruct a lost civilization.

Mrs. Apodaca, perhaps, was the only one in all Santa Fé who took the news calmly. She went about all day serenely wrapped in the folds of her shawl. She seemed to be pondering a highly amusing thought. Her big brown eyes twinkled and her lips were set in a quirk of secret laughter.

"What is so amusing about the bomb?" I asked, out of all patience.

"It is amusing, Señora, that so terrible a thing should be made where it was made. No?"

"At Los Alamos?" I asked bewildered. "Where the sons of the *ricos* went to school?"

Mrs. Apodaca shook her shawled head. "No," said she, her eyes shining. "On the Pajarito Plateau. *Pajarito,*" pronounced Mrs. Apodaca, rolling her R and separating her syllables.

Then the meaning of the Spanish word dawned on my literal Anglo intelligence. That world-shaking bomb was born, not only within hailing distance of ancient, buried civilizations. It was born on "the Little Bird Plateau."

That Atomic Oven

MRS. APODACA, stubby whitewash brush in hand, strode purposefully through my yard early one morning. I knew from the way her shawl was bound firmly under her chin that an unusual need for money had arisen in *Casita* Apodaca.

She stayed her resolute steps long enough to offer a few words of explanation. "It is that Carmencita," she laughed, a bit ruefully. "She thinks she must go Girl Scouting this summer. So I must work eight days at four dollars a day for the new Anglo on the *Camino*. Eight days I must work that Carmencita may sleep in a tent and eat food around a smoky campfire like a barbarian."

But the next day, Mrs. Apodaca did not stride through my yard. After a while the new Anglo, who had built a fine house on the *Camino,* called. "What has happened to Mrs.

Apodaca?" her voice shrilled over the telephone. "She promised to work eight days for me. And I have every labor-saving device to make it easy for her."

In an effort to defend Mrs. Apodaca's customary integrity, I promised to investigate.

No one was around *Casita* Apodaca. Mrs. Vigil came from a neighboring blue-painted door at my repeated knockings.

"Ah, Mrs. Apodaca, she now works for the old one, the Doña Estefanita. She was not content in the fine house of the Anglo, on the *Camino*." Mrs. Vigil pursed her lips as if she might tell many things if she were not the essence of discretion.

It was almost a month before I saw Mrs. Apodaca again. She came to the Little Adobe House laden with the spoils of her long labors for the old one—iris bulbs, geranium cuttings, paper roses, and hand-pounded chile paste. She looked unusually bright-eyed and cheerful. Evidently her work had not been too strenuous.

Patiently I waited while she rocked back and forth in the big rocker. At last: "Ah," breathed Mrs. Apodaca, "that Doña Estefanita has a nice house. Two hundred years old it is—

water from a good well, nice coal-oil lamps, little fireplaces in every room and a wood stove to cook on." Suddenly Mrs. Apodaca stopped rocking and sat up straight. Her big eyes flashed, as she added, as wrathfully as her gentle voice permitted: "And not one what you Anglos call the device to save the labor—not even an atomic oven.

"Ah," said Mrs. Apodaca, smiling with happy memories, "every wall in that big adobe of the Doña Estefanita I whitewashed with my own good brush, and then I rubbed them down with a piece of sheepskin. They glisten, those walls, Señora, like snow with the sun on it. And her lambs' wool mattresses and pillows I tossed and pounded on the sunny *portal*. Soft and fluffy as little clouds they are now—those mattresses. And I buried her Indian rugs in the last dry snow we had and then I swept them with a good stiff brush. You should see how their colors came back. And the elegant lace curtains of the Doña Estefanita I washed and starched. Stiff as icicles are those curtains, not limpsy (excuse it please, Señora) as the Anglos like their curtains."

"But Doña Estefanita pays only two dollars a day," I protested. "You had to work twice

51

as long to make the Girl-Scouting money for Carmencita."

"*Sí*," agreed Mrs. Apodaca, unconcerned, "but I have a happy time. I work for the Doña Estefanita in peace, Señora. No roaring of vacuum cleaners! No pop-pop of spray guns! No calamity with the atomic oven."

"Atomic oven," I puzzled.

"*Sí*," nodded Mrs. Apodaca, "it cooks without the help of the human head or the human hand."

"Oh, automatic oven!" I exclaimed.

"*Sí*, atomic electric oven," agreed Mrs. Apodaca easily. "Ah, that was a terrible day I worked for the new Anglo on the *Camino*. Of course, out of politeness I could say nothing. All I could do was to disappear and never go back. I could not hurt her feelings, Señora."

Again I marveled at the native idea of courtesy, whose "*sí*" so often means "*no*."

"The Doña Estefanita and I took a two-hours *siesta* each day," continued Mrs. Apodaca. "And when we were weary with whitewashing and mattress beating, we sat in the shade of the cottonwood tree and made red and pink paper roses for her vases, and cut out flowers from pieces of red flannel to float in the oil of her glass lamps."

"Didn't the Anglo on the *Camino* like your stubby whitewash brush?" I asked.

"She had," snorted Mrs. Apodaca, "what she called a device to save labor, a spray gun that exploded whitewash over everything—the *vigas,* the ceiling and me. There was no controlling it. And the dust bag of the vacuum cleaner was stuffed with dog hair. She has two collies. Two hours it took me to clean that dust bag.

"And then the new Anglo went away and left dinner cooking in the atomic oven," whispered Mrs. Apodaca, rolling her eyes and coming to a climax. "While I was up on the stepladder trying to wipe the whitewash splatterings from the *vigas,* the Anglo called on the *teléfono.* She was beside herself. She had set the atomic oven for high instead of low. Señora, for some time I had been smelling burning food, but who am I to question an atomic oven? The rest of the day I spent cleaning burned food from that oven."

Mrs. Apodaca sighed as she pondered darkly the incomprehensible. "A whole day I worked, Señora, cleaning the devices to save the labor so that they may labor again. *¡Verdad!*"

Quaint
Miss Boggers

"HOW QUAINT,"
visitors ejaculate, as they wander about the narrow, high-walled streets of Santa Fé. "How Old-Worldish, how charming!" They stop in their tracks and stare with delight at black-shawled women, trudging (if the truth be known) prosaically toward the grocer's and the day's improvident purchase of a minute wedge of cheese and three yellow onions.

For a long time I thought it was the Anglo heart that was starved for quaintness. But now that I have observed the fascination Eudora Boggers has for Mrs. Apodaca, I am inclined to believe this starvation is universal.

Eudora Boggers slipped quietly into Santa Fé and bought, at an outrageous price, a crumbling adobe studio in the dirt road district. That district is the mellow fringe of urban Santa Fé, given over almost entirely to the golden-walled little houses of our Spanish-American citizens and the aping adobe citadels of Anglo artists and writers. Quite definitely, the dirt road district has atmosphere. It possesses quaintness. It is a kind of adobe Olympus.

Santa Fé and other art centers know numerous women like Eudora Boggers. They are women who have spent long years competently doing social work, teaching school, or taking dictation. No one dreams, as the strident years go by, that these women live in a world of their own devising. They refer to it vaguely as, "When I Have Time To Do All the Things I've Wanted To Do."

Past middle age, some of them retire or come into a modest inheritance. Pell-mell they rush for places like Santa Fé. Arty berets perch on graying curls. They may be seen in Tenorio Flat, blissfully seated before new easels, somewhat uncertainly copying Mr. Archuleta's goatpen. Or they wander at sunset on the color-dyed hilltops, mumbling recalcitrant verses. Always mentally I salute these women. Once I, too, lived in the land of "When I Have Time To Do All the Things I've Wanted To Do."

When Mrs. Apodaca, who works only occasionally a carefully estimated number of hours to cover an unusual family expense, took to working three days a week, month in and month out for "Mees" Boggers, I was amazed. As regularly as clockwork, Mrs. Apodaca stalks through my yard in the morning and returns at nightfall, filled with gentle gayety and dramatic incidents.

"Does Miss Boggers paint?" I asked.

"No," Mrs. Apodaca acknowledged regretfully. "No, she does not paint the pictures, but she wears what she calls a smock."

"Maybe she writes poetry."

"No," said Mrs. Apodaca, slightly on the defensive, "but she wears what she calls a beret."

"Maybe she studies Spanish."

At this, Mrs. Apodaca shrugged her shoulders. "Not from a book. Sometimes when I am dusting or sweeping, Mees Boggers will say, 'How does one say in Spanish, "a bird in the hand is worth two in the bush?"' All day she will talk to me in strange Spanish about the bird in the hand and in the bush.

"Yesterday," confided Mrs. Apodaca, "Mees Boggers had company, two fine ladies from her home city, which is a place called De Troy Ett.

You should have seen the *casita* when it was all ready."

I could picture, without seeing, that *casita* of Miss Boggers. Into it would be crammed everything typical of the country—hand-carved furniture, tin-framed mirrors, Chimayó blankets and Navaho rugs, Mexican pottery and Indian bowls. It would rival the local museum.

"It was a warm day," Mrs. Apodaca confessed, "but Mees Boggers had a piñon fire in her fireplace. The ladies from De Troy Ett wore fine, heavy, wool suits. Mees Boggers wore her *fiesta* skirt with the rows and rows of red 'reeka-racka' braid and her blue velveteen Navaho jacket. And she wore all the silver and turquoise jewelry she has bought—beads and necklaces and earrings and so many bracelets they played a little tune.

"After a little while Mees Boggers said to bring in the *merienda*. That *merienda,* Señora, I do not think the ladies liked. Against all I could say, Mees Boggers gave them hot Mexican chocolate in her pottery cups, which always taste a little of the soil of Mexico, and some of my blue corn *tortillas.*

"What with the heat from the fireplace and the hot chocolate and the melted butter dripping from my blue corn *tortillas* on their fine blouses, the ladies soon said they must return to their hotel.

"When I opened the blue-painted door for them, one of them looked at me and whispered to Mees Boggers, 'How quaint, how very quaint.' Señora, what is quaint?"

"Quaint," I explained, hunting for words Mrs. Apodaca would understand, "is something that seems strange only to the eyes of the person looking at it—strange and lovely at the same time."

Mrs. Apodaca pondered the thought with complete absorption. At last: "Ah!" she exclaimed, "I thought the lady from De Troy Ett was looking at me. But, *verdad,* she must have been looking at Mees Boggers. She is the most quaint person I know."

There was a long silence. "Except you, Señora," added Mrs. Apodaca loyally.

Concerning Koshare

THE LAST NIGHT of Santa Fé's *fiesta,* Koshare came to make his home in the Little Adobe House, which is not complete without a cat. Cowboy, his immediate predecessor, had departed for greener pastures. Coming back from the Candlelight Procession, over dark hills, I stumbled over a kitten huddled on a flagstone in the shadow of my wild plum tree.

"He needs a home," Mrs. Apodaca assured me. "Mrs. Vigil's white cat has three or four more. Such families as that white cat has!"

There was little white about the mite of kitten sitting round eyed in the palm of my hand. His long, soft fur was striped irregularly around his body in jet black and good, sun-tanned adobe russet. On his forehead was a scattering of dashes such as the Indians use to symbolize raindrops. He carried his fluffy tail like an Indian Rainpole and spread over his shoulders was the Thunderbird in full flight.

I named him Koshare, after the clowns in Indian dances, the bringers of laughter, the Delight Makers. But there all resemblance to the calm, earth-serene Indians ceased. Through the months, Koshare's Tenorio Flat origin has asserted itself. He is as gay and Latin-hearted as a lilting guitar.

The Tenorio Flat influence was first demonstrated in his food. Not for Koshare were bowls of creamy milk from my neighbor's yellow cow. Neither was he a meat eater. Like the people in the little adobe houses, Koshare liked red beans cooked with onions and pungent with chile. Squash, rice, and stewed celery were among his favorites, with canned corn the peak of gustatory delight.

Unlike Cowboy, his predecessor, Koshare takes no responsibility for the household he graces. The Little Adobe House being built in the form of an L, it is often difficult to hear the telephone bell or someone tapping at the front door. Cowboy always summoned me at such times, his serious face dented with furrows of concern. As far as Koshare cares, people can knock their knuckles off at the door, and the only interest he has in the telephone is to knock the receiver off and down to the floor with a terrible clatter in the dead of night. As I am on a party line, this greatly upsets the little Spanish-American operators in our telephone office.

Cowboy did not approve of company in the Little Adobe House. Coats and galoshes spread about the room upset his ideas of order. He would look from the disorderly array to me, pucker his face and signal me tight-lipped, "We never put galoshes there."

As the fire leaps in the corner fireplace, as candles throw delicate shadows against plain, white walls, and laughter and happy voices fill the room, Koshare puts on a show that soon makes him the center of the gathering. He runs pell-mell up and down the room, he sails like a flying squirrel from chair back to chair back. He stands on his hind legs and makes wild passes at flickering shadows.

Should he be forgotten in a rising tide of conversation, he has another trick that always regains his star place in the company. He starts to put out candles. With dexterous, well-aimed pattings, he extinguishes their flame. In spite of the smell of burned fur and the disconcerted gasps of the guests, Koshare puts out every candle in the room until we have no light but the blazing piñon logs.

Cowboy was a literary cat. He served as a break for too lush adjectives and too whimsical flights of imagination. The instant the typewriter was uncovered, he took his position on the dictionary. Here he knotted his forehead and watched with concern every word typed. "Do put your mind on this and try to write something of some profundity," he seemed to say.

Koshare, I fear, has no literary sense whatever. In fact, I believe he reads the funnies. Typewriter keys are charming objects to grab when in motion, and manuscripts make fine tearing noises when slyly pushed to the floor and torn to ribbons: "Why write about sun on adobe?" beguiles Koshare, working at the door latch and swinging on yellow print curtains. "Come on out and soak it up."

Cowboy enjoyed radio programs, particularly the early morning news. Koshare likes only the Spanish hour given on the Santa Fé station. Spanish songs, Spanish music set him flying about the room in an overflow of joy and abandon.

Like Mrs. Apodaca, Koshare loves flowers. Wild gooseberry blossoms in an orange pitcher, plum blossoms in a dull blue vase, engage his delighted attention, evidenced by blissful sniffings and purrings. He is quite meticulous not to nibble my cherished house-plants, unless his supply of vegetables has been limited. Then he chews a geranium leaf in lieu of a salad.

In my deep-set flower window is a dwarf chile plant with waxen green leaves and inch-long scarlet peppers. For all their small size, the little peppers are much more piquant than the large ones used for cooking in Tenorio Flat. Day by day my little peppers are disappearing. Koshare, true to his early environment, is eating them, one by one, in spite of gusty sneezing and watering eyes. Lovable, carefree, and gay, something of Tenorio Flat moved into the Little Adobe House along with Koshare.

Mañana
Is Tomorrow

EARLY EVERY
morning in the year, the musical song of Mr.
Apodaca's axe drifts rhythmically from Tenorio
Flat. In summer it is a brief song. Mrs. Apodaca
needs but a few sticks of piñon wood for the big
iron cook-stove which perfumes her corner of the
Flat with entrancing odors. But, as the days
shorten and the yellow leaves drift from the cottonwood trees, the song of the axe lengthens
gradually until one morning I can say without
looking out, "Snow today."

Mr. Apodaca's early morning wood-cutting
moves my Anglo neighbors to smug comments.
"Shiftless," they exclaim, conscious of their own
neatly stacked woodpiles and overflowing baskets
by the fireplace. "No foresight." And they think
it serves Mr. Apodaca right to go out in the snow
and struggle with piñon wood in a howling wind.

But, according to his thinking, Mr. Apodaca has not been improvident. Quite early in the autumn, he borrowed his *primo's* truck and made several trips to the mountains to bring home piñon logs in five-foot lengths. These are neatly piled in an angle formed by the house wall and the shed of *la cabrita,* the goat. But the reducing of those logs to the right proportions for *mamacita's* cook-stove is a day-to-day operation nicely calculated to the temperature and the cooking needs of the family.

To see Mr. Apodaca, topped by a bright-red knitted cap and grown suddenly stout in a sheep-skin jacket, is to see a man who is in tune with his early morning work. His big, dark eyes sparkle. He sings a little monotonous song in rhythm with his cadenced axe. *"La nieve*—The snow," he sings. *"Hoy mismo*—This very day."

Anglos explain almost everything they do not understand about their Spanish-American neighbors with the word *"mañana." "Mañana,"* they say, smug in their own activity and fretful care. They do not know that Mr. Apodaca belongs to a timeless race. *Mañana* is not the essence of his philosophy, but *hoy mismo* is. Yesterday, for him, stretches back hundreds of years. Tomorrow is not his concern. But *hoy mismo*, this day, is his. It is a matter of emphasis.

"How do you manage always to have carrots and lettuce coming along in your garden?" I ask Mrs. Apodaca. "I always forget to replant until my rows are almost gone."

Mrs. Apodaca smiles the wise, benign smile of a sibyl as she pulls the yellow carrots from her adobe soil. She unties a corner of her shawl to show me a pinch of carrot-seed tied snugly in a knot. For each carrot she pulls, she drops a seed from the store in the corner of her shawl. "When I pull, I plant," she explains gently, "in the same hole. *Hoy mismo.* This very day."

During the war years, all of us had known for weeks that Miguelito Apodaca was to leave on a certain date for a training-camp in "Tehas." One-half hour before his bus was to leave, Mrs. Apodaca sent me a letter by Carmencita.

"*Estimable* Señora," wrote Mrs. Apodaca in her best Spanish flourishes. "Miguelito has no suitcase for the going to camp. If you have one you do not need, we make happy to pay you what is right."

I dashed out to the garage, grabbed the first suitcase I could lay my hands on and ran at top speed to *Casita* Apodaca. The place teemed with relatives and friends gathered to say *"adiós"* to Miguelito. I was the only breathless one in the entire company. Bowls of chile and platters of *tortillas* were circulating calmly.

Mrs. Apodaca inquired in detail as to the well-being of my household. Then she presented me to each of her guests. She produced a battered purse. "Whatever is right, Señora."

"It only took up shelf room," I gasped and made a hurried exit. Five minutes later, there was Carmencita at my door again. *"Mamacita wants* you to have it," she said, extending a wrapped package. Inside was a bright-red pillow top, woven on the hand loom that stands by Mrs. Apodaca's sunny window. The finest of wool had been woven into a scarlet square and in the center was the Thunderbird, done in turquoise and brown.

With her son leaving for camp, with a house full of guests, Mrs. Apodaca did not wait to say, *"Gracias."* This very day, almost this very minute, she said it with the work of her own hands.

Solution of a Problem

WHEN MIGUELITO Apodaca brought his California wife and two little boys to Santa Fé to live, he did not have to start hunting frantically for a roof over their heads. A snug new addition to the Apodaca *casita* awaited their arrival. It held out strong, welcoming brown arms and was decorated with a red geranium, blazing like a candle on the front window sill.

The Apodacas and other residents of Tenorio Flat are blissfully unaware that they have solved for their small community a world problem—the housing shortage. It all started during the war. While the rest of Santa Fé awaited permits and materials for building, Tenorio Flat was swinging its whitewash brush over new adobe walls and painting a turquoise-blue trim around square-paned little windows.

Tenorio Flat, which is supposed to be the essence of things *mañana,* had not only solved its own housing shortage, but had solved it first. It stood expanded (a bit out of line), ready to receive returning sons and daughters, *primos* and *amigos.* While anxious Anglos dashed from commission to commission and from lumber yard to roofing man, the Apodacas and the others of Tenorio Flat were starting piñon fires in new fireplaces and rejoicing in additional outside wall space to cover with drying chiles.

It all started early in the spring before Victory. How Tenorio Flat knew at that time that a few months would bring most of their sons and daughters back with new husbands and wives is a mystery. Perhaps, living so close to the good adobe soil, they knew, as the piñon jay knows the time for nest building.

As soon as frost was out of the ground that spring, Tenorio Flat, to a man, got out its long-unused frames for making adobe bricks. Every yard rattled with the sieving of sand and the slap-slap of the mixing hoe. Out of the abundance of their adobe soil came their building material.

Soon long rows of adobe bricks were drying in the sun. All the men left in the Flat held jobs down town, but after hours, they reverted to their ancient skills and made bricks as if they had all, at one time, been the most be-spattered of adobe men. They worked as long as there was one flicker of daylight left along the rim of the Jemez Mountains.

Later in the summer, when the bricks had dried, walls began to spring up like magic. Higher and higher they rose, until, by the end of war, there was *mañana* Tenorio Flat on top of the world and its own flat roofs.

Then such a house-cleaning as went on! Out into back yards walked ornate iron beds that usually ranged end to end up and down the sides of rooms. No color was bright enough for their re-painting. Lavender beds, salmon-pink beds, chile-red beds blossomed like grotesque flowers in all the back yards.

On sunny *portales,* mattresses were emptied of their lambs' wool stuffings. Mrs. Apodaca and Mrs. Vigil bound their heads with flour sacks and knelt with a slender wand in either hand. Such a tossing and a lifting as the heaped lambs' wool received. The kneeling women, with white bound heads, bent over their work, the rhythm of the slender rods rising and falling, the flight of pigeons caught in a wedge of sunlight gave the scene something of the beauty of a Grecian frieze.

But when Miguelito and his family arrived, Mrs. Apodaca was suddenly overcome by misgivings. Wrapped in her oldest shawl, she stared gloomily at the little houses scattered helter-skelter over Tenorio Flat. "That wife of Miguelito," she said darkly, "maybe she think we live like barbarians in our little mud houses. They do not live like that in Los Anhelees. I saw when I was there."

"Nonsense," I tried to cheer her, "the wife of Miguelito will love the little mud houses."

But Mrs. Apodaca shook her head. "I like them and you and Mees Boggers like them. No? But young girls from a big city, maybe not."

"Artists like them," I protested. "There is a lovely painting of our little mud houses in our Art Gallery now. Why don't you come with me to see it?"

It was sheer despair that forced Mrs. Apodaca to see that painting. As usual, there was a crowd around the picture of little adobe houses on a snowy hillside. Blue shadows lay along the snow, and golden wings of sunlight spread along their walls.

Mrs. Apodaca stood, swathed in her shawl, and looked and looked. At last she said, "It is pretty." And then wistfully, "I would like to buy that picture for the wife of Miguelito."

I glanced at the price list. "The artist is asking seven hundred dollars," I said. Just in time I caught Mrs. Apodaca's swaying figure.

But the next morning she was singing as she drew water from the well with the bright blue cover. As I glanced at the new additions to the *casitas* of Tenorio Flat, I chuckled to remember how it had solved a world problem with ancient skills and solved it first. Such is the power of *hoy mismo*.

The Belle of the Baile

MRS. APODACA and the other residents of Tenorio Flat meet the big problems of living with quiet dignity and endless patience. It is over the minute and trivial matters that they chatter like nesting birds and flutter from house to house for prolonged and dramatic consultations.

When Mrs. Apodaca glided, full speed, into the Little Adobe House early one morning, I knew by the way her shawl was bound tightly under her chin that one of the lesser problems was upsetting her usual calm.

"Señora," she burst out, without the usual inquiry for my health, "will you, *por favor,* save all your eggshells? Break them only through a little hole at the end. I am going to need dozens and dozens of eggshells."

"Are you going to color them for Easter?"

I asked. "Are the *muchachos* going to have an Easter egg hunt?"

"No, no, Señora. I make *cascarones* for the Easter *baile*. Ball."

"*Cascarones?*" I questioned.

"*Sí*," Mrs. Apodaca nodded breathlessly. "When the eggshells are dried, Armendita, Carmencita, Lupe, and Luz will fill them with pieces of colored tissue paper, pink, blue, and yellow, and then pour in a few drops of perfume and seal the opening. At the Easter *baile* the boys will break *cascarones* over the heads of the girls they ask to dance. The girl who has the most colored paper in her hair will be the belle of the *baile*."

Mrs. Apodaca twisted the big turquoise ring on her index finger and smiled wistfully. "I want Mary-Ho, the wife of Miguelito, to have the most colored paper in her hair. I want her to be the belle of the *baile*. I want dozens and dozens of *cascarones* for Miguelito and his friends to break over Mary-Ho's head."

Mary-Ho, the pretty wife Miguelito had brought from Los Angeles, had been named María Josefina, as befitted her Spanish-American parentage. But long years in public school had changed it to Mary Jo. Her mother-in-law had accepted Mary in place of María, but her tongue could not manage the English J. So the wife of Miguelito had become "Mary Ho" to all Tenorio Flat. The name had a fine exuberant sound.

"That Mary-Ho," sighed Mrs. Apodaca, "never says a word, but I am afraid she finds Santa Fé very slow. In Los Anhelees they often went to fine dances and to the *cine* and rode down to the beach on Sunday in an *automóvil*. That is why I want her to be belle of the *baile* at her first dance in Santa Fé."

I promised to use eggs with profligate abandon. Already I was planning a menu of omelettes, custards, and sponge cake.

"That Mary-Ho has a like-Hollywood dress to wear that she brought from Los Anhelees," Mrs. Apodaca flung back over her shoulder as she hurried homeward.

A few days later Armendita appeared with another problem. *"Mamacita* has decided to go to the *baile*," she said. "Don't you think, Señora, that she should wear the new dress she bought to go to Los Angeles last year? Never will she wear it. It just hangs up on a hook against the wall."

I remembered, with a catch in my heart, the sight of Mrs. Apodaca in the cheap blue dress, its hem let out until it reached half way to her black-cotton-stockinged ankles and her high, laced "comfort" shoes.

"What does *mamacita* want to wear?"

"Oh, her best black dress, that is so long it reaches the floor, and her Sunday shawl with the silk fringe, and her big gold earrings," sighed Armendita. "Not one thing stylish."

"Armendita," I said sternly, "your mother in her long black skirts and her fringed shawl and her big earrings is the most beautiful lady I know. Let her wear what she wants. After all, she will just sit in a chair and watch." Thus, in weighty disputes and profound conferences, did the *baile* of the *cascarones* approach.

About mid-morning of the day following it, Mary-Ho came running full tilt into the Little Adobe House. From the glow on her pretty face I knew the *baile* had been wonderful.

"Never," exulted Mary-Ho, "have I had such a time. It was simply super. You should have heard the guitars and the fiddles and the singing. And such good things to eat spread out on long tables. And showers of colored paper from the *cascarones!* And the air filled with perfume! Oh, it was fun! All morning I've been brushing paper out of my hair and dress."

"Then you were the belle of the *baile!*"

"No," laughed Mary-Ho. "I had lots of *cascarones* broken over my head, but I wasn't the belle of the *baile.*"

"Who in the world was?"

"*Mamacita,*" giggled Mary-Ho. "You see, after they had danced all the new dances, old Don Ignacio and a lot of older *caballeros* wanted to dance some of the old dances. They tried Lupe and Luz and all the younger girls. But none of them could do them very well. Then Don Ignacio marched right up to *mamacita* and broke three *cascarones* over her head. You should have seen them do *La Varsoviana.* It was like a floor show. *Mamacita's* skirts blew out around her and her shawl streamed out behind her like a banner. Everyone was watching and clapping and throwing flowers. The minute she and Don Ignacio had finished, up rushed all the older *caballeros* and simply mobbed *mamacita. Cascarones* broke all over her."

A Matter of Emphasis

ANGLO neighbors kept dropping into the Little Adobe House after my return from a long vacation. During my absence, one trouble after another had evidently descended on the Apodaca family.

There had been two terrific thunderstorms that had turned into veritable cloudbursts. During the first one, the Apodaca roof had caved in completely and, during the second, the house had turned into a kind of cistern where household goods floated, dank and waterlogged.

Then the dress shop where Armendita earned good wages had been sold and she had been unable to find other work.

Out in the green valley of Chimayó, where Mrs. Apodaca's relatives have fragrant orchards watered by meandering little ditches, a late frost had wiped out the apricot and cherry crops.

Then her parents' adobe had caught fire from a defective chimney, and roof and supporting *vigas* had gone up in flame. Only the blackened adobe walls were left. Mr. Apodaca, in a midnight dash to his fire-beleaguered parents-in-law, had run off the road and wrecked his dilapidated car beyond repair.

As I hurried over to Tenorio Flat to offer neighborly concern and support, I pictured Mrs. Apodaca swathed in her oldest shawl to the eyebrows, a sibyl of despair amid the ruins of her home and fortunes.

But Mrs. Apodaca was not swathed in any shawl. Her head was covered with a white flour sack and she was perched high on a rickety box. As she slapped the whitewash brush against mud-stained walls, she was singing in a tone of deep content:

> Chula la mañana,
> Chula la mañana,
> Chula la mañanita.
>
> Beautiful the morning,
> Beautiful the morning,
> Beautiful the early morning.

"Ah, Señora," she greeted me, eyes shining through a freckling of whitewash spatterings on her brown face, "it is sad that you had to be away when Santa Fé was most beautiful. After the fine rain the Río Santa Fé was running brim to brim and all the little deetches were singing with much water."

"But your poor roof," I reminded.

Mrs. Apodaca laughed and fluttered her brown hands in careless dismissal. *"No importa,"* she said lightly. "A roll of tar paper, eight inches of adobe soil and we have a fine new roof. Now I make the walls shine with fresh whitewash. See, Señora, I have fixed the little window for the summer."

The deep-set little front windows of Tenorio Flat are a kind of domestic display case. Mrs. Apodaca had arranged a summer display that consisted of a large pottery deer with branching antlers, a blossoming begonia, two highly-colored cups and saucers, and a glass lamp that twinkled with much polishing. I was sorry that the silk handkerchief I had brought her could not be stood up with the rest of the treasures. But Mrs. Apodaca was not to be foiled. Quickly she transfixed it through the center with a large safety pin and hung it to the edge of her new side curtains.

"But Armendita," I persisted, "it is too bad she lost that fine job in the dress shop."

"*No importa,*" beamed Mrs. Apodaca. She lowered her voice, "confidentially, I think a little later, Armendita marries Manuel M. Morelas. He comes from a family of weavers in Chimayó. Right now, Señora, I invite you to the wedding."

"But your relatives' orchards—the cherry and apricot crops"—

"*No importa,*" Mrs. Apodaca brushed the calamity aside. "Are there not peaches, pears, and apples, as well as wild plums, left?"

"But the *casita* of your parents and the fire that took the roof?"

"*No importa,*" repeated Mrs. Apodaca. "They took the wood-wagon and went up to the mountains for new pine tree *vigas.* With the tar paper left from our roof and eight inches of adobe, they, too, have a fine new roof."

"But Mr. Apodaca's car?"

"*No importa,*" declared Mrs. Apodaca.

"See, Señora, we saved the seat and put it under the wild plum tree. That *carro*, Señora, always the *gasolina*, the flat tires. Now we can sit on the seat under the wild plum tree in peace and not think of the *gasolina*."

It was no use. My neighborly concern was wasted. Mrs. Apodaca dismissed five major disasters as lightly as if they had been so much fluff from the cottonwood trees.

But a few days later, gloom like a dense fog swept down over *Casita* Apodaca. Then my neighbor swathed herself in her oldest shawl and refused to see any of her friends who tiptoed to her door. Even the children went about long-faced and silent. After almost a week of mysterious grieving, Mrs. Apodaca wandered wanly through my yard.

"Can't I help?" I offered, pitting myself against the unknown.

"No, no, Señora," replied Mrs. Apodaca sadly. "No one in all the world can ease my heart." At this she put her hand dramatically in the general vicinity of that harassed member.

"If you could only tell me what has happened."

"Ah, Señora, I have told no one, although

the chattering *muchachos* will tell it to all the world. It is Carmencita. The schoolteacher said a terrible thing about my Carmencita."

"What in the world could she say about Carmencita?"

"She said," whispered Mrs. Apodaca, "she said that my Carmencita makes flat when she sings."

Cousin
Canuto

SCATTERED along the outskirts of Santa Fé, scarcely noticed by Anglos, are many little grocery stores. They are the Latin version of the country store that flourished a generation ago along the Atlantic seaboard. Usually these *tiendacitas* occupy the front room of some adobe dwelling. Here the "improvident natives" may come at all hours of the day and night, even on Sundays and holidays, to buy three eggs for breakfast, a box of soap powder for the family wash, or cookies with blue marshmallow frosting for social gatherings.

The little stores have a warm, endearing quality. Around them the life of the store-keeping family flows in homely rhythm. *Mamacita* wheels the baby buggy in beside the fat wood-burning stove and waits on customers, while *papá* goes to the wholesaler for a crate of pink soda pop. Onions, strands of red chiles, and wood smoke give the place a distinctive fragrance. The *muchachos* stop in for penny candy. Shawl-draped neighbors come in for three onions and a wedge of cheese, and stay all morning for a chat and a steaming cup around the stove. The credit system consists of slips of paper impaled on a row of nails—a nail each for the Apodacas, the Vigils, and the Escuderos. The cash register is a small wooden box.

Urban Santa Fé has its modern markets and shining chain stores, all elegance and efficiency. In one of them worked Cousin Canuto. Mrs. Apodaca was as proud of Cousin Canuto as I would be if a cousin of mine were ambassador to the Court of St. James. Cousin Canuto stood behind the counter of a serve-self market. He checked purchases and rang up one's total expenditure on a great shining machine that added up with a rattle and disgorged a final slip of paper for the customer's dismay.

Cousin Canuto is a native in whom the ancient Spanish strain has persisted. Even in his immaculate white apron and jacket, crossed by a watch-chain like a gilded ship's cable, Cousin Canuto gives the impression of a gentleman of high degree in the silks and satins of Velásquez.

In addition to his romantic aspect, Cousin Canuto can discuss the price of cabbages in three languages—his own flowing Spanish, my English, and the pueblo-dwellers' monosyllabic Tewa. His long, beautifully shaped fingers handle the intricacies of the monster cash register as an organist's produce symphonic strains from a keyboard.

Mrs. Apodaca delicately spread the report, throughout Tenorio Flat, that Cousin Canuto received the unheard-of honorarium of two hundred dollars a month. At that, he was underpaid, it seemed to me. Cousin Canuto could send you out of the serve-self market with mundane paper sacks of groceries piled to your chin. But you left with the feeling that you were a great lady, engaged in important affairs.

Suddenly a red-headed boy from Texas was behind Cousin Canuto's counter. Cousin Canuto had simply disappeared. Mrs. Apodaca wrapped herself in gloom and her oldest shawl. Cousin Canuto's name was never mentioned again. Evidently the Apodaca pride had been punctured in a vital spot by whatever calamity had happened to the famous cousin Canuto.

Months later, at nightfall on a snowy Sunday, it seemed that nothing but toasted cheese crackers, eaten before the corner fireplace would be appropriate. From long association with Tenorio Flat, I, too, had become improvident. There was not an atom of cheese in the house.

A little jaunt through a snow-packed world would increase my zest. But, alas! blue grocery doors that opened so willingly to belated taps at night can be closed as easily. Mr. Alarid had left a pencilled note at his place of business: "I go dance in Cundiyó." If Mr. Alarid had gone to dance in Cundiyó, then every other local storekeeper had also gone and I resigned myself to cheeseless crackers.

Back in the gathering darkness of my yard, I almost ran down little Tiofila Quintana, a box of corn flakes under her *mamacita's* shawl. "Wherever did you find a store open," I asked.

She pointed vaguely toward the snowy hills. Then, seeing that I knew of no store in that direction, she slipped a brown hand in mine and led me up along the ditch where snow was heaped in an unbroken trail. Taking an icy path I had never noticed, we emerged into a *placita* where lamplight shone from a dozen windows in a nest of little houses. *"Allá,"* pointed Tiofila [there] and scampered homeward.

For a moment, I hesitated to open the door she had indicated. The rhythm of three guitars, one fiddle, and a lusty chorus of *"Allá en el Rancho Grande"* were seeping out. When I did go in, I saw a fat, round iron stove blushing red with blazing piñon logs. Around it, in addition to the musicians, were three baby-buggies containing Murillo cherubs, attendant *mamacitas,* shawl-wrapped and shadowy, a dozen children spread out on the floor with dogs, cats, and a yellow rooster, and two old men whittling indefinite objects.

In the midst of the lamp-lighted, stove-glowing room, in the midst of good peppery and wood smoke fragrance, stood Cousin Canuto. He looked ten years younger. As he wrapped up a small wedge of cheese for me, he glanced delicately at the row of credit nails along the wall. "Perhaps you would like to pay at some later time?"

As I put down the small change, he tossed it negligently into the small wooden box. "Be seated, Señora," he begged, waving me toward a backless chair by the stove. "It is a good night to sing, with all the world so quiet and still outside."

Three guitars, one fiddle, and the chorus, with Cousin Canuto in the lead, rolled joyously into "El Rancho Grande."

The Fountain
of Cousin Canuto

AFTER Cousin Canuto recklessly left his fine job with the serve-self market to operate his own *tiendacita,* his Señora, María Lupita, and Mrs. Apodaca often had their shawled heads together. The despair over Cousin Canuto's foolishness grew darker with each discussion.

"To think," mourned Mrs. Apodaca, "a man with seven *muchachos* should throw away two hundred dollars a month, that he might fill his credit nails with bills from half the neighborhood and sing 'Rancho Grande' on winter nights! Now that summer is here, he sings more than ever," she complained. "Like a bird, he sings. And, when he is not singing, he carries pails of water from the well to water his hollyhocks. It is *'mamacita, por favor,* watch the store while I draw water for the hollyhocks.'

"María Lupita, *poprecita,* must take her hands from the washtub and wrap up three onions and a slice of cheese for Mrs. Archuleta. She must leave her frijoles to burn upon the stove, to take a penny from Agapito Alire for an all-day sucker. Ay, and for what, Señora? A man with seven *muchachos* to feed must spend his days watering hollyhocks and singing!"

But, one day, Cousin Canuto's prestige returned in even greater glory than when he played tunes on the great cash register in the serve-self market. He built a fountain in the center of his *placita.*

"Have you seen the fountain of my Cousin Canuto?" Mrs. Apodaca asked. In her eyes and voice was the old-time pride. "You should see it, Señora. It is *magnifico.* People are coming from far and near to see it. From Agua Fria Street, they walk; and they even drive in from Chimayó and Chupadero. Ah, that fountain!"

Thus urged, I hurried up the path beside the waterditch and thought how unfortunate it was that it turned in its meanderings in a direction that left Cousin Canuto's *placita* without its singing benefits. Surely, anyone who loved flowers as Cousin Canuto did, should have more than buckets of water drawn from a well to refresh them.

A crowd of chattering admirers milled around what was evidently the fountain in the center of the sun-baked *placita*. But the hollyhocks drew my attention away. The little flat-roofed house stood in a veritable forest of them. Scarlet, rose, yellow, magenta, and white, the silken blossoms ran up thick stalks that reached for the blue sky. Their beauty was the more startling in that the rest of the *placita* was bare, hard-packed adobe.

Not for the Spanish New Mexicans are the Anglos' green lawns and flower borders. In early days, water was too scarce for such luxuries. "We sweep our yards," Mrs. Apodaca once explained. Even the youngest toddler in a family soon learns to grasp a broom twice as high as itself and sweeps the packed adobe around the house.

That hard-packed, much-swept adobe around the little houses, built from the same substance, is surprisingly attractive. The good bulk of house-walls falls in lovely shadows on it. *Vigas,* protruding beneath the flat roof, add long irregular oblique lines to the design.

When the group around the fountain had thinned a little, I approached Cousin Canuto's latest and greatest triumph. "Ah, Señora," he greeted me, "you come all this way on a hot morning to see my *fontana?*"

In the center of the sun-bitten *placita,* cut in geometric designs by sun and shadow of thick walls, stood a fountain shaped like a miniature Pyramid of the Sun, in Old Mexico. Along its triangular sides, little pockets had been gouged out to hold thick-leaved succulents. Between the green, growing plants, bits of colored glass, blue, green, and amber, had been embedded in the cement-like adobe. They caught the sun and twinkled like the facets of a jewel.

An iron pipe came out of the pyramid's tip and around it unfolded the petals of a sunflower, skillfully fashioned from flat pieces of tin. At the base was a tin-lined basin to catch the water from the pipe. In truth, it was a masterpiece!

"That sunflower," Cousin Canuto explained his artistic difficulties, "was hard to get right. At first I painted it bright yellow *como* nature. But it did not please me. After many days of deep thought, I decided to paint it blue—blue like our sky and our turquoise stones and the feathers of the piñon jay. If people wish to see a yellow sunflower, they can see a thousand along any roadside. But a blue sunflower—that is something beyond and above. ¡*Verdad!* As you can see, it is now perfect, Señora. It lifts the heart."

Men removed their broad-brimmed hats and shook Cousin Canuto's hand. Women rolled their eyes heavenward in speechless admiration. Children hopped up and down in sheer joy. At last, Cousin Canuto was a citizen of distinction again!

Back in the Little Adobe House, my mind was filled with Cousin Canuto's statement of something "beyond and above." Perhaps he had voiced, better than the learned experts, the essence of art. Later, an arresting thought terminated my peaceful musings. No water spouted from Cousin Canuto's fountain. It could not, because no piped water was within a mile of his *placita.* Even the "deetch" water was far away. The only water that magnificent and famous fountain would ever see would be a bucketful laboriously drawn from the blue-hooded well.

Hybrid Casita

SOMETIME
last year, an Anglo family moved into Tenorio
Flat. It was the first of its kind, but housing was
scarce. A squat little adobe under silver maple
trees was vacated by the Escudero family, who
moved back to one of the villages in the shadow
of Truchas Peak.

Santa Fé has few restricted districts; we live
cheek by jowl in our thick-walled little houses.
Mrs. Apodaca put on her best shawl and presented the Anglo family with a geranium plant
she had coaxed into crimson bloom through the
long winter months. Mrs. Vigil sent a stack of
blue corn *tortillas* and a bowl of red beans with
grated cheese.

But the Anglo family remained decidedly
alien in the midst of friendly Tenorio Flat. It
can happen in Santa Fé, where Anglos are a

minority group. All one has to do to realize this strange state of affairs is to thumb through our thin telephone directory and to roll the sonorous Spanish names on the tongue—Gallegos, Gurulé, Gomez, Gonzales, Griego, Guerrero, Gutierrez.

Many people living in cities in today's uproar have cast longing eyes on the peace and simplicity of Tenorio Flat. One lady wrote asking for the first vacancy. She said she would be content with the smallest and most primitive of houses, but she must have a garage big enough to accommodate her Cadillac.

There is scarcely a garage in all Tenorio Flat. A few families have dilapidated *Fordcitos,* but they are hardy contraptions and stand out winter and summer. The high point of any winter morning is to get the motor unit of the Flat thawed, dug out, and started toward waiting jobs. Sometimes it takes the entire male population until almost noon.

The Anglo family did not seem to appreciate the high points of life in Tenorio Flat. For all they were only renting, they fell upon the little house with many novel improvements. Plain whitewashed walls were tinted the latest in pastel shades. Venetian blinds went up at the windows. Broadloom carpets covered the floors and the hum of a vacuum-cleaner mingled with the morning pat-pat of brown hands spatting out tortillas and the song of Mr. Apodaca's axe. A truckload of overstuffed furniture was moved in. In no time at all, the little house looked like a stout peasant girl togged out in the furbelows of the latest fashion.

The new Anglo stopped me one day. "We want to call our house 'The House of the Big Maple Trees,'" she said. "How do you say it in Spanish?"

"*La casa de los*"—and then I couldn't think of the Spanish word for maple. As I started to run back to consult my Spanish dictionary, the Anglo stopped me.

"Never mind," she decided; "we'll call it '*La Casa de los Maple Trees*.' There's too much Spanish around here anyway."

So that strangely hybrid name was painted in black letters on the wall back of the *portal*. Mrs. Apodaca's geranium sickened and withered behind the Venetian blinds. Mrs. Vigil's *tortillas* and beans were discovered in the garbage pail. Complaints were filed with the city authorities against twanging guitars and dancing feet that often enliven late winter nights. The small son of the new family was discovered throwing rocks at Koshare as he perched on the top of my squat, warm chimney.

Through it all, the residents of the Flat went about smiling blandly. They were punctilious in doffing broad-brimmed hats in greetings. There was scarcely a ripple on the surface of the accustomed calm. But, knowing Tenorio Flat, I was sure that something gentle, but decisive, would happen.

It did. Suddenly the Anglo family moved away. Mrs. Apodaca's Miguelito and Mary-Ho moved into the little house. Mrs. Apodaca went over daily, armed with her stubby whitewash brush. Soon all the pastel walls were back to their comfortable white again. The Venetian blinds were sold to the second-hand man. The geranium put out new buds and the hybrid sign on the *portal* was painted out with three coats of turquoise blue.

It was several months later before I knew what had actually happened. Then one day, Miguelito picked me up in his *Fordcito* and gave me a lift to the plaza. "So you and Mary-Ho are renting the Escudero house," I said.

"Not renting, Señora; we buy it."

Knowing the inflated value of even the smallest of adobe houses these days, I wondered how a young day laborer had found money enough to make even a down payment.

"Everyone in Tenorio Flat brought money," laughed Miguelito. "Fifty dollars, twenty-five dollars, ten dollars! Even one dollar from the old one, Señor Gurulé. I have a good job now driving a milk truck and Mary-Ho is doing some housework. Soon we can pay them all back. But they say they don't want it. If they don't, we will give a fine *baile* this summer.

♦

That Carmencita

MRS. APODACA
sat limply in the big rocker before my corner
fireplace. "That Carmencita," she complained.
"It was bad enough when she made flat when
she sang. Now I wish she do nothing but sing."

Carmencita is not like any other child in
Tenorio Flat. She has shot up into a long-
limbed bundle of energy with a strange assur-
ance for a twelve-year-old. In a community of
little girls with carefully contrived curls, much
like bed springs, Carmencita now contents
herself with a thick thatch of bangs to her eyebrows and a smooth braid fastened with bits of
bright yarn filched from her mother's weaving.
Member of a race which can see no virtue in the
Anglo skill of salesmanship, Carmencita can sell
anything.

"A fine concert by the school orchestra,"

she says dreamily, as if she heard, even then, the cadences of strings. "I've saved you a couple of tickets. Only a dollar each plus tax."

Month after month I bought tickets for school concerts I never heard and track meets I never saw—tickets for rummage sales and puppet shows. When, at last, I rebelled, Carmencita gave me that understanding, almost compassionate glance of hers. It said as plainly as if she had spoken, "I'll find something she will buy."

In a short time she was back with a vast assortment of greeting cards embellished with violent colors and saccharine verse. There was not a single occasion of human living that did not have its appropriate card. "And I got you enough stamps to send them all out with," murmured the enterprising salesperson.

Greeting cards in time gave place to gadgets—can openers that would take a degree in engineering to operate, and rubber heels for home shoe repairing. It was a happy day for me when Carmencita turned her attention to contesting. Over the radio, in stores, and in strange publications she found contests. She named new products. She told in twenty-five words or less why she liked a certain soap, soup, or syrup. She collected boxes, cans, and bottles with trade names, against a possible contest and the need for evidence of her purchase of the same.

Her long legs were always whisking down to the wooden mailbox on the cross street. This in itself was unusual, as Tenorio Flat pays little attention to its row of mailboxes, for the simple reason that there is seldom anything in them. By her long face and somber eyes I judged that the contesting was not going too well. But suddenly, she won a full-size bedspring. As there was no mattress to go with it, it still is standing on end in Mrs. Apodaca's weaving room, waiting for a mattress contest.

Carmencita has developed baby sitting to the point of professional standing in Santa Fé. "I have a long waiting list," she says modestly. I learn of her ability from Anglo mothers who vie for her services. Her charges are tucked in bed on the minute and go to sleep immediately. They do not waken to ask for so much as a glass of water. This gives the sitter opportunity to wash any dishes left in the kitchen, which most sitters ignore. It also gives her long hours to scan the magazines of the household from which she culls news of more, bigger, better contests.

Boarding with a family in Cousin Canuto's *placita* is an aged, English-speaking native who is considered practically a millionaire as he receives a state pension for the blind. At Carmencita's instigation, he hired her, at twenty-five cents an hour, to read to him three hours a week after school.

Mrs. Apodaca sought my help on this latest activity. "I go to the school PTA, Señora, and they say we must know the books our *muchachos* read. How can I know when I cannot read English?" Being curious myself, I wandered up to the *placita* and saw the old, big-hatted man and Carmencita propped against a warm adobe wall. I did not need to look at the book. The words of "Treasure Island" came floating out on the sun-filled air. Later it was "Robinson Crusoe" and then "Gulliver's Travels."

After a while, when anything unusual happened in the neighborhood, the people exclaimed: "That Carmencita!" Mrs. Apodaca was torn between pride and apprehension.

Last winter, Tenorio Flat became one vast quagmire of adobe mud, due to snow falling on snow, melting, and adding mud to mud. As few of the Flat children owned galoshes, great were the complaints of *mamacitas* and school-teachers over mud-tracked floors. *Papás* were driven to call timidly on city officials for a few loads of gravel to spread over the twisting roads. But nothing came of it.

One morning I noticed Carmencita leading a dozen or so children schoolward. To my horror, she was leading them through the worst puddles and pools. They were caked to the knees with red adobe mud. The very next morning big trucks lumbered into the Flat and spread a deep layer of red gravel everywhere. "That Carmencita," everyone chuckled.

A schoolteacher gave the facts. "It is a rule in our school," she explained, "that tardy pupils go to the Principal's office. Carmencita's group was tardy. On the Principal's office floor are two fine old Navaho rugs. Carmencita was most considerate. Not one child put a muddy foot on the rugs, but he thought they would. He hustled them out, and spent the rest of the morning talking persuasively over the telephone."

Carmencita has started a new book with the big-hatted native in the *placita*. It is entitled "Careers for Women."

The Battle
of the Mailboxes

FOR A GOOD many years, the mailboxes of Tenorio Flat huddled together on a forest of weatherbeaten stakes along the nearest cross street. Some of them were little wooden boxes in which laundry starch had come. Some were rusty tin containers which had once held coal oil. A few were battered affairs, bought in the dim past at the Five-and-Dime. Perched on their wobbly supports, they looked like a flock of disreputable birds.

No one paid much attention to them. Occasionally the disgruntled mailman stopped his car and deposited an impersonal communication of some kind. It usually turned grey with age before any one picked it up. Communication in Tenorio Flat is largely by the spoken, not the written, word. If you have anything to say to people who live out of town, you take the day

105

off and go to see them. The custom has its excellent points. It includes a holiday, hours of enjoyable, unhurried conversation and a good chile-fragrant dinner. There is no mountain of unanswered correspondence to reproach the eye in the adobe houses of Tenorio Flat.

This idyllic situation continued until "that Carmencita" became a woman of affairs. Then the old starch box of the Apodacas held important missives. What with the contesting, the small merchandise Carmencita sold from door to door, and the free samples of commodities she ordered in great variety, the old mailbox suddenly came alive. Twice a day Carmencita rushed down to the road to collect her correspondence or to await anxiously the slow progress of the mailman up the hill. The look of intentness on her thin, big-eyed face was a new note in Tenorio Flat.

Then out of her accumulating capital, Carmencita subscribed for the local daily paper and had it sent to her by United States Mail. No uncertain delivery boys for Carmencita!

Mrs. Apodaca felt it necessary to explain such unheard-of extravagance to all her neighbors. "That Carmencita, she theenk," explained her mother, baffled but loyal, "that she need that paper for her school work—curren' events she call it."

Almost immediately, Carmencita had the "Curren' " events class completely demoralized, her teacher told me. She referred glibly to the FEPC, CARE, the ERPC, and the AEC. She went alphabetical so rapidly that neither pupils nor teachers could follow her. Soon Mrs. Apodaca was talking in portions of the alphabet and, as she gave all the letters their Spanish pronunciation, her conversation became even more cryptic than that of her daughter. A Rosetta stone was sorely needed in Tenorio Flat.

Enterprise usually entails the expenditure of more capital. Evidently Carmencita drew on her liquid assets. A fine new rural free delivery mailbox appeared among the starch boxes and coal-oil cans. It stood firmly on a new stake and had two little flags. It attracted a good deal of attention. On its side was an identifying card with "CARMENCITA APODACA" in large capitals and underneath, in far smaller letters, "and family." Carmencita wore the key thereto on a stout metal chain secured to her dress pocket by a safety pin.

Tenorio flat is not the place to take such blatant ostentation sitting down—especially from a *muchacha*. Unlike Carmencita, the other residents, having no liquid assets, were forced to draw on their skills and imaginations. Señor Vigil, who is something of a wood carver by avocation, constructed a mailbox that people came from miles around to see. The box was small, as befitted a family which did not indulge in correspondence, commercial or personal. But its facade was decorated with a reproduction of the head-dresses the Indian women wear in the Green Corn Dance. It was beautifully carved to represent square-topped mesas and was painted to show cloud, rain, and snow responding to the plea of the dance.

Within a few days, not to be outdone, Señor Archuleta responded with another mailbox, on which perched a carved and painted piñon jay, wings outspread as if for instant flight. At least a dozen other mailboxes appeared, one by one. Each one was visited by crowds of admirers. Carmencita's shining new box received no attention whatever. What was worse, neither did Carmencita.

With a master stroke, Carmencita turned

defeat to victory. No one goes near the mail-boxes now—not even the mailman. Carmencita has rented a lockbox in the post office down town. It costs her two dollars a quarter and she has to walk a mile to the plaza each day to collect her mail. The key to the lockbox hangs on a chain about her neck. It seems to be a kind of talisman to restore her to her rightful place in Tenorio Flat. It is well worth all the trouble and expense.

Mrs. Apodaca summed up the whole situation alphabetically one evening, "After all, Señora, you cannot go higher than the central *oficina* of the U. Esse. Pe. O.," she remarked, wagging her head.

*Por Nada –
It Is Nothing*

MARGOT,
the etcher, who has a little adobe house not far
from Cousin Canuto's sunny *placita,* also had a
studio in New York City. For several years she
shuttled back and forth from one extreme of
living to the other.

But a day came when Margot decided to go
entirely New Mexican. "I'll have to go back
and sell and ship my studio things," she deter-
mined. "How I'd like to take this last look at
the great city through the eyes of a child."

That was the way Tomasito, Cousin
Canuto's twelve-year-old, happened to go to
New York. Tomasito had never been further
away from Santa Fé than the Pecos River. He
had never ridden on a train. He had never slept
in a hotel. He had never eaten in a restaurant.

Most of the year, Tomasito padded barefooted through the warm adobe dust of Santa Fé. Ragged blue overalls, and a faded shirt comprised his costume. Summer and winter he went hatless, his long, wavy hair raying out like a nimbus about his head.

Margot gave Cousin Canuto's Señora a generous bill. "Take Tomasito down town and buy him whatever clothes he needs," she instructed. "But let him pick them out himself. I don't want to take a poor imitation of an Anglo boy along with me."

Cousin Canuto's Señora understood. The result was that Tomasito started on the great adventure clad in long trousers of a bright Taos blue. Shining black shoes were on his feet. But the crowning glory was a superb leather jacket that zipped from chin to waistline. Within and without, it held many pockets, all restrained by zippers. It was magnificent.

For a hat, Tomasito chose one as nearly like Cousin Canuto's as he could find—a broad-brimmed, low-crowned black felt to be worn on the back of his head. His taste seemed to center on hand-carved leather, with a wide belt around his waist and a narrow one around the crown of his *sombrero*. He also bought a little comb in a carved leather case and a money wallet big enough for a captain of industry.

That wallet was worthy of the son of Cousin Canuto. Although Tomasito had not so much as two battered coins to rub together, he invested a large portion of his clothing allowance in a prodigious wallet. It had places for lodge and identification cards, a capacious coin purse, and a roomy place for bills of all denominations. The whole contraption had two zippers, one within and one without, against the loss of valuables. To see Tomasito seriously zipping first the inner and then the outer security fasteners of his empty wallet was to see a fabulously wealthy little boy.

But the empty wallet soon contained five crisp one-dollar bills, all of which Tomasito accepted with grace. He likewise accepted the American metropolis with aplomb. The streamliner, the dining-car, the towering buildings, the taxis, the sight-seeing trips, Tomasito accepted with beaming delight, but quite in stride.

He bought many things to take home to the sunny *placita*. There were small replicas of the Statue of Liberty, and mechanical toys that cavorted violently around the hotel room. But, significantly, the high spot of the adventure was not Radio City, not the Aquarium, nor the zoo nor the great busses, but a human being: Anton.

Anton was a waiter in the café Margot frequented. He was so dignified and correct, so of the old school, that he could take a small boy's order for hamburger steak and two fried eggs without so much as a flicker of his well-schooled features. He had imagination enough to bring unasked a jar of red preserved cherries to decorate a mound of white ice-cream.

No matter where they might be at meal-time, they had to return to Anton's table even if the city had to be crossed. Anton listened with controlled amazement to talk of Indians and cowboys. In the midst of exciting explorations, Tomasito would suggest, "Let's go see Anton."

Their last dinner with Anton was almost a ceremony. When it was finished farewells were sadly said. Coats were put on. But Tomasito hesitated. Anton was standing, the image of the perfect waiter, beside his serving-table. "I have something I want to give Anton," said Tomasito, moving toward his friend.

He approached the perfect waiter and drew

the enormous wallet from a secret pocket of his leather jacket. He held it in his brown hands as he carefully unzipped first the outer and then the inner fasteners. There was an intense frown between his big brown eyes. People at nearby tables stopped their meal to watch.

Tomasito put something in Anton's hand. Margot, who was waiting at a little distance, heard Anton's tone of violent protest. "Oh, no, no! I couldn't accept that."

Then she heard Tomasito's clear young voice above the din of the room.

"*Por nada,*" he insisted, lapsing into his local idiom, "it is nothing." It is what one says if one is thanked for a favor or a gift—"*Por nada*—it is nothing."

With a dismissing gesture of brown hands and with great dignity, Tomasito rejoined Margot. It was not until they were on the train that she found out what he had given Anton. "Twenty-five cents," exulted Tomasito. "I saved it on purpose." With the air of a Croesus, he carefully zipped his empty wallet, both within and without, and stowed it away in the hidden recesses of his leather jacket pocket. He zipped the pocket.

Compliment
For a Lady

ALL THE
muchachos around Cousin Canuto's *placita* call
Margot, *La Grandota*—The Very Big One.
When a circus came to Santa Fé, *La Grandota*
packed nine children into her ancient *Fordcito.*
The three youngest ones she took on the seat
with her, the six oldest she crammed into a kind
of fish-wagon affair in the rear. As she packed
more and more exuberant *muchachos* into the
car, they screamed in the composite language
they are developing, that is neither Spanish nor
English, *"Pusha-le, pusha-le."*

At the circus grounds she unloaded the
uproarious youngsters to the roared advice of
"pulla-le, pulla-le." Then she led the blue-over-
alled army through the animal tent. In the
hands of the six oldest *muchachos* she placed
one ticket of admission to the main tent, one

ticket of admission to the concert, and one to the Wild West show. To this was added a fifty-cent piece for each one to buy his favorite refreshment in the shape of ice-cream cones, popcorn, and all-day suckers.

Tomasito, who had braved the complexities of New York, was placed in charge of this contingent. "Look around awhile," Margot said. "I'll take the *chiquitos* in to our seats. But the minute you hear the band playing for the grand entry, come right along in with us. And don't let go of your tickets," she cautioned.

Ambrosio, Simonito, and Juanito, all under five years of age, she led to reserved seats on the lowest row, where weary short legs could reach the good adobe earth. In the excitement of buying red and orange balloons and of recognizing friends and neighbors as they found seats, time ceased to exist. Piping voices squealed: "*Mira, mira*—look, look! Pantalones, all the way from Trampas. *Hallo*, Pantalones. *Mira, mira*, Juan, from Chama! *Hallo*, Juan."

But not a word from small Ambrosio, not a single *mira* or *hallo*. After all, three and a half years was rather young to see a circus. Margot wished he would reassure her with just one faint *mira.* He sat like a small Latin edition of the Sphinx, his eyes growing bigger and his long lashes raying out in stiff amazement.

Before they knew it, there was a blast of music and the grand entrance parade moved gorgeously around the ring. Simonito and Juanito were one shrill chorus of delighted *miras.* But Ambrosio sat rigid and silent.

Where were the older boys? Margot wondered. They must not miss the first acts. Propping the *chiquitos* together and charging them not to budge an inch, she hurried toward the entrance. She had to dodge a cageful of lions and a dozen beautiful ladies on horseback.

There at the entrance stood Tomasito and his five charges. They stood as if rooted to the spot, glaring at the man who took tickets. "Hurry, *muchachos,*" Margot urged. "The show has started. Why didn't you come in?"

Tomasito drew himself up in outraged dignity. "The Señor there," he nodded coldly at the ticket-taker, "would not let us in without our tickets. *Grandota,* you say, 'Hold on to your tickets!' We hold on to them."

Margot snatched tickets from clutching brown fingers and marched her stiff-backed *muchachos* to their seats and a re-united party. Now the *mira, mira* uproar never stopped. She was nudged and pulled in all directions to see trapeze artists flying through space, to see lions leaping through rings of fire and seals balancing red balls on their noses.

Only Ambrosio sat without making a sound, his big eyes following all that was going on. If he would only let loose with one *mira,* Margot fumed. If this keeps on, he will go pouf like an exploded balloon.

When it was all over, when the concert had been applauded with rhythmic stampings, when the last bronco had bucked his way out of the Wild West show, the *muchachos* made a final round of the animal tent. A lion roared obligingly. A giraffe extended his incredible neck. Camels chewed their tethering stakes. But not a word from Ambrosio!

To crys of *"pusha-le,"* the *Fordcito* was reloaded. Suddenly Ambrosio leaned against Margot's shoulder. Pointing a fat finger at the elephants in an outside paddock, he uttered the first words of the afternoon. *"Mira, mira,"* he shrilled, *"muchas, muchas, grandotas"*—[many, many very big ones].

Innocent and Quiet Minds

THE ONLY room in all Tenorio Flat that I have ever seen carefully locked is the door to Mrs. Apodaca's weaving-room. Otherwise, the citizens of the Flat emulate the Arcadians and have "neither locks to their doors nor bars to their windows."

Many years ago Mrs. Apodaca built her weaving-room, almost single handed, out of scraps of lumber and discarded adobe bricks. It had one large window and a tiny door fastened with the biggest padlock I have ever seen.

On snowy afternoons, it is good to pass Mrs. Apodaca's weaving-room and to hear her contented song in rhythm with her busy shuttle.

But the weaving stopped for a while when one of the older married girls, Paz, came from "Tehas" with her own little two-year-old daughter. In that child, as in Cousin Canuto, the old

Spanish thread had reappeared in startling distinctness and beauty. Her skin was a warm ivory, her eyes as limpid as a fawn's, and her eyelashes so long and thick they looked artificial. Curls of dark brown lay in glossy waves on her mild forehead.

"Blanca," Mrs. Apodaca informed me, trying to conceal her pride. Some days later, in talking with Paz, I mentioned with joy the small and very Latin Blanca. Paz laughed. "Blanca, that is not her real name. It is what you Anglos call a pet name that *mamacita* gave her. I gave my baby a stylish Anglo name. Her real name is Priscilla. It makes a nice name—no?—with my husband's family name, Priscilla de Baca."

Not in my wildest imaginings could I picture the small Priscilla in home-spun gray crossed by a white kerchief. Rather, I always pictured her in twirling *fiesta* skirts and red slippers, with a rose behind her ear.

During Paz' extended visit, Mrs. Apodaca took the opportunity to visit her relatives in Chimayó. Paz would care for the Apodaca household and, in her spare minutes, weave a blanket to take home for the admiring gaze of her husband's people.

But alas! after her mother left, the key to the enormous lock on the weaving-room door could not be found. *"Mamacita* promised to leave the key by the pottery deer in the window," Paz worried, "but it isn't there. I've hunted the house over."

But a few days later, I heard Paz' young voice mingling with the song of the loom and was glad that the key had been found.

In mid-October, Mrs. Apodaca returned in the farm-wagon of a big-hatted relative. Like a shawl-wrapped goddess of the harvest, she sat on the farm-wagon floor surrounded by a New Mexican gleaning. *Ristras* of red, waxen chiles spread about her like a crimson sea. Indian corn, yellow, blue, purple, and red, tied in bunches of five, heaped the corners. Pumpkins and little golden squashes rattled about. There were sacks of dried peaches and apricots and a brown jar filled with goat cheese.

Mrs. Apodaca barely greeted us before she was hanging her chile *ristras* against the brown, sunny walls of her *casita*. Corn, pumpkins, and squash went up on the flat roof. In clear autumn sunlight from a bright blue sky, *Casita* Apodaca took its rightful place in the New Mex-

ican landscape. It blended with the splashes of
aspen gold on nearby mountains and with the
yellow exclamation-points of poplar trees close
at hand. They and the scarlet chile *ristras*
repeated the colors of the ancient banner of
Spain.

Mrs. Apodaca looked about her with content. *"Es bueno* to be home," she said and
suddenly clutched a corner of her shawl. "I
forgot to leave the weaving-room key," she
lamented to Paz. Tied in a tight knot in the
shawl's corner was the key. "I am sad to think
you couldn't get your blanket woven."

Paz shook with laughter. *"Mamacita,"* she
chided, "long ago, when I was a little girl, you
often would say on a cold winter night: 'Paz, *por
favor,* run out and see if the weaving-room door
is locked!' Always you thought of that big lock
in the middle of the night when I would have to
leave my snug bed.

"Look, *mamacita,* this big lock has never
really worked—not for years and years. See, the
part you press down never clicks. It just goes
into the opening and does nothing."

Mrs. Apodaca examined the big lock
closely and her face fell. All the years she had

been sending her children from their warm beds to see if the weaving-room was locked! All the years she had gloried in the big padlock and carried the key safely tied in a corner of her shawl!

"Never mind," comforted Paz. "Tomorrow I go down town and buy you another padlock, the biggest I can find."

"No," decided her mother with emphasis, "we spend the money for something better than padlocks. Tomorrow I go downtown and buy a pink silk bonnet for little Pre-see-la to greet her *papá* when she returns home."

Then she added: "If I think the door is locked all these year. it is locked. If *todo el mundo* [all the world] thinks the door is locked, it is locked. *¡Verdad!*"

Little John Biscuit

THE MOST
endearing quality of my neighbors in Tenorio
Flat is their love for children. When Mrs.
Apodaca summons grubby, shock headed, fat
little Dado at close of day, *"Angelito,* Little
angel," she calls.

No matter how many *muchachos* may
crowd the little adobe houses, the last baby is
always a dazzling marvel. Early in the spring, I
noticed a crowd collecting around the Vigil
casita. Men, women, children, including big boys
of high-school age, were gathered in intense admiration about something I could not see.

"Some boy has a new bicycle," I thought,
as I joined the crowd. But it was not a
new bicycle. It was Mrs. Vigil's seventh grand-
child spread out on a pink satin pillow in the
arms of his mother.

This love for children, which even adolescent boys evidence, is more than a fleeting emotion. It means a big boy with a small brother's hand in his on many a manly expedition. It means a small girl, directing the progress of three or four toddlers. It means a place of welcome for any homeless child. It means hours of work in Anglo kitchens to buy Easter outfits for every child in the family.

It means gentle guidance. Seldom have I heard a child screamed at or beaten in Tenorio Flat. One year when Dado kept breaking off the buds of his mother's cherished irises, I asked her if she never spanked. "Why, Señora, I am beeg and he is very little," she answered aghast. Most corrections are whimsical and highly humorous. General laughter often follows them. The result is soft-spoken children with an odd dignity and grace that comes from knowing they are much beloved.

Even when Cousin Canuto's Juanito had our end of town in an uproar for most of a summer's afternoon, there were no recriminations. One of the older *muchachos* dashed madly past the Little Adobe House. Shortly afterwards, he returned followed by Mrs.

Apodaca, binding her shawl about her throat in a gesture I have learned to know means dire emergency.

"It is Cousin Canuto's Juanito," she shouted over her speeding shoulder. "That three-year-old has been lost two hours now. No one can find him."

Little, fat, big-eyed Juanito lost! I, too, soon hurried up the path beside the water ditch to Cousin Canuto's *placita*. Where could a three-year-old disappear to from that populous center?

I joined the solemn party that searched each neighboring house. Bare little two- and three-room places they were, without cupboards or nooks or crannies. We looked hopefully under beds and peered into wash tubs. No Juanito!

The hard-packed adobe yards were equally bare—no clumps of bushes, no barns, no hay-mows. Every blue-hooded well was carefully screened with chicken wire. Where could Juanito hide himself in such a bare, open place? While the others hurried down the dusty road, I paused by the famous waterless fountain to make one final survey of the immediate vicinity.

Over in one corner of the yard was an unused, out-of-doors bake-oven, made of adobe. It was conical in shape, something like an over-sized beehive. Before the baker's product had become popular, it had baked the bread for all the neighborhood.

I hurried over and stooped down to look into the small curved opening. There, on a pile of drifted autumn leaves and the charcoal of long-ago fires, slept Juanito. A cherubic smile was on his peaceful, rosy face. His thick, black bangs stood up like rabbit's fur and his long lashes were black against his cheeks.

The returning search-party streamed over at my beckoning. Not a word was spoken as, one by one, they stooped down and looked into the beehive oven. Something in the excitement of the moment awakened the sleeper. Calmly he crawled out of his snug hiding place on hands and knees, like a little, fat cub. Still not a word from the crowd around the old oven. With great dignity, Juanito stood erect on his short, fat legs. His face and clothes were daubed with ashes and charcoal. Dry leaves clung to his hair.

Everyone waited for the culprit to get

used to his surroundings. There were no clutchings, no questions, no frantic embraces. Everyone stood smiling broadly while Juanito got his bearings; then he trotted over to the shadow of his mother's long black skirts. A smile, like a sunrise broke over his soot-daubed face. He was home again.

Cousin Canuto's eyes twinkled. "Juanito *bizcocho*—little John Biscuit," was all he said. Laughter rippled through the crowd. The children took up the refrain and made a song of it.

> Juanito, Juanito,
> Bizcocho, bizcocho.

they sang, dancing around in circles.

Probably, when Juanito is playing on the school football team, or later when he is running for office in the strange politics of our state, he will be known affectionately as Juanito Bizcocho, son of Canuto, singer of songs and builder of famous fountains.

Cousin Canuto's
Grandfather

EXCITEMENT ran like a tide through Tenorio Flat and spread to every cluster of adobes in the vicinity.

"Would you believe it, Señora," Mrs. Apodaca asked, tieing knots in her shawl fringe in abandon, "the *abuelo* — grandfather — of Cousin Canuto, is going to visit him here. Not for forty years has that Old One been in Santa Fé. Not in all that time has he been far from his village in the mountains. Only a raveling of dirt road leads to that village, and there everything remains much as it was when I was a *muchacha*."

Cousin Canuto was beside himself with the drama of the occasion. "Ah, Señora, *mi abuelo* will think he is in another world. What will he think when he sees Los Alamos and learns what they make there? What will he think when he sees a hundred *automóviles* whirling around our plaza? We are planning an all-day picnic at the airport. What will he think when the big planes from the ends of the earth drop down there as lightly as a bird? Ah, Señora, it ties the mind in tangles."

The *abuelo* of Cousin Canuto arrived at last in Santa Fé. Had he delayed another day, all the flat roofs would have blown off with suppressed anticipation. Cousin Canuto, trying hard to conceal his pride, brought the old one almost immediately to the Little Adobe House.

Never had I seen such a handsome old man—tall and erect in his new blue overalls and homemade shirt. He swept his many-angled *sombrero* from his head and called down blessings on my *casita* and me. Grace, dignity, and serenity entered my room—not an old man.

Cousin Canuto fluttered about, showing off the modest wonders of the little house. "*Mira, abuelo,*" he demonstrated with flying fingers, "you set this little box on the wall and the Señora may have any amount of heat she wants, day or night. She may go away and when she returns, her *casita* will be just as warm as she told the little box she wanted."

The old one smiled benignly, but his eyes wandered to the white, corner fireplace. "I see that the Señora also has the small *fogón*. Ah, when one sits by an open fire of piñon wood, there is warmth for more than the body. The heart also knows a radiance. *¿Verdad?*"

It was the plaza that most intrigued the old one. Day after day he sat on a bench, munching piñon nuts, his big hat pulled over his wise old eyes. Everytime I went downtown, I stopped for a little chat with him.

As cars fought for parking and passing space, he chuckled. "In my day, Señora, it was the wood-haulers, with their burros, who circled the plaza. What a man was a wood-hauler! He belonged to an honored calling. What do the wood-haulers, with their trucks, get out of their calling these days? So many dollars a week to buy more *gasolina* for the truck to haul more wood to buy more *gasolina*. It goes on without end.

"Work, Señora, should leave something with which one can decorate one's life. I still have much pleasure in remembering the days when I led my sheep to high mountain meadows. I was a *pastor* [shepherd]. I have forgotten what I bought with the little money I earned, but I can close my eyes and see the little fire I built at night in the midst of the blackness, and hear the songs I used to sing to keep me company."

On the last night of the old one's visit, Cousin Canuto gave a party in his small store. All the neighborhood overflowed the building and the hard-packed adobe outside. Two fiddles and three guitars strummed and lilted hour after hour. Voices were lifted in the old songs, and feet tapped out the old measures.

To many questions, the old one replied politely, "Ah, I have seen many wonders in Santa Fé—the great birds that fly, laden with people, to the ends of the earth, the *cine* that laughs and talks, the electric wire that turns night to day, the *automóvil* that runs in swarms like ants up and down the streets. It is all a wonder."

"Then Santa Fé has changed," insisted Cousin Canuto. "You can tell the people in the village how it has changed."

132

"Ah, but only on the outside," nodded the old man. "Inside everything is the same." He nodded toward María Josefina Archuleta, with her baby in her arms. He glanced out of the open door at the stars in the dark-blue New Mexican sky. He lifted his voice in "La Golondrina," which the young people were singing. "Everything that matters stays the same," said the old one, with deep content in his voice.

I could see that Cousin Canuto was quite cast down.

Lady
On a Palfrey

DURING
our long summer evenings in Santa Fé, the
surrounding country shows a strange eruption.
From dozens of tangled footpaths, children
come running, chattering, and skipping, bound
for the early shows at the movies. Little
boys in much-washed, blue overalls, their
hair sleeked back in shining arcs and triangles, descend upon the town in packs, like
exuberant puppies. Little girls in red, yellow,
and blue dresses, float like blobs of pigment
down the hills, along the little water ditches.
So numerous are the children and so rapid
their pace, I get the impression that they are
not *muchachos* at all, but color and flight
converging on a central point.

Sometimes I am able to distinguish a
familiar face or step in the evening flight,

but not often. "That Carmencita" is the only one who seems at all real. Which, perhaps, is because she usually rides a bicycle, a very old bicycle bought by way of much baby sitting, canvassing, and contesting.

Due to her many activities, Carmencita always starts late for the movies. I would see her intent, serious face bent low over the handlebars, her long legs pumping like pistons, her eyes fixed on the distance she must cover to reach the movie on time. It was always a false note to pass Carmencita movie bound. In the midst of color and flight, she was off key.

Then, one evening, I met her trudging movie-ward on her two hurrying feet. As usual, she had allowed herself scant time to cover the distance. As usual her face was tense and her eyes fixed on the distance ahead. "Where are your wings?" I asked.

"*Mamacita* won't let me use my bike," she tossed back over dogged shoulders. "Too many *turista* cars on our narrow streets."

After that, I met her many times hurrying along. Never was she with a group of her own age. More often she was urging along a crowd of small Archuletas and Vigils, much as a shepherd hurries sheep across a highway. And, I knew, tightly clutched in Carmencita's fingers was money for her own admission ticket, cannily extracted from *mamás* and *papás* for her services in shepherding.

For some time I have had a concern for Carmencita. How could Mrs. Apodaca's daughter turn every occasion into money-making? Where along the short trail of her life had she lost the Spanish grace, the disdain for money-making, the delight of giving? What had she done with the romance that permeates even the most humble of her peoples' small affairs?

I should have known better! The first inkling I had that the old graces were intact in this child of Mrs. Apodaca, the *prima* of unworldly Cousin Canuto and no one knows how many hopeless romantics, came from Sabina Vigil, who is a kind of Tenorio Flat walking newspaper. "Carmencita doesn't walk to the movies any more," informed Sabina.

"So her *mamacita* is letting her ride her bicycle again," I observed.

"Not her bicycle—but she rides," said Sabina, and disappeared around the corner.

Immediately I had visions of a boy school-mate who possessed one of those contraptions consisting of four wheels and a snorting engine, which affluent *muchachos* buy, tinker with, and occasionally coax into running. Such transportation would be entirely in keeping with Carmencita's modern tendencies. Or it might be a youth with a decrepit motorcycle and Carmencita perched precariously behind him. To the tune of a wide-open exhaust, they would dash to the movies. That picture seemed even more fitting than the ramshackle, stripped-down car.

Then one summer night of great loveliness, with a new moon hooking a finger over the edge of dusky mountains, I met Carmencita en route to the movies. Truly, she was not walking! Her way was a queen's progress and a medieval queen's at that.

A great clumping sway-back horse passed me. On its back sat a youth topped by a low-crowned, black felt hat with a leather thong holding it under his chin. His shirt was brightest silk, his trousers black and tight fitting to the ankles. Up their outer seams little silver buttons twinkled in the half-light. He looked like a gallant horseman from the Argentine.

It was young Mr. Abeyta, who no longer lived in Tenorio Flat. Behind him on a folded blanket and sitting sidewise was Carmencita. Her hair was out of its long braid and had been curled at who knows how great a cost. Beyond the curls and shining eyes, all I could see was a form wrapped in a white silk shawl with the longest fringe of any shawl in the region.

They were not hurrying. They were not talking. They were acting a part on a stage whose backdrop was the dusky mountains and whose lights were the fingers of new moon and the windows of little adobe houses. They might have been Sir Galahad and the Lady Elaine. They might have been Don Quixote and the fair Dulcinea.

The Old
Adobe Maestro

NOT SINCE
the war has the Little Adobe House experienced
a good plaster job on the outside. The fire walls
along the flat roof were badly crumbled and
there were holes up and down the sides. Something had to be done.

All my Anglo friends recommended a
cement job over the mud bricks. "It will last
forever," they advised, "and you can paint it
to look like adobe." But adobe houses, covered
with even skillfully-painted cement are not
adobe houses. They lose their gentle contours
of roof line and wall curve. They lose the
charm that is inherent in the indigenous and
the hand-wrought.

Julio, the old adobe *maestro* of the Flat,
is in great demand. Only by speaking far ahead
and obtaining the intercession of Mrs. Apodaca

did I obtain the services of the maestro. The minute frost was out of the ground, Julio was at my door. "I can work eet," he exclaimed. "Get a load of sand and I start *mañana*."

Considering Julio's many years and the weight of buckets filled with moist adobe mortar, I thought to suggest a youthful helper, but hesitated in the face of Latin pride. "Maybe I better have helper," he said of his own accord. "Work go faster and helper get only seventy-five cents an hour. My boy makes good helper. I bring my boy."

Within twenty minutes, Julio was back with "my boy" for the amenities. His name was Ambrosio and he was stout and middle aged. We shook hands and inquired for each other's families. Then great activity whirled around the Little Adobe House. Shovels, hoes, and picks appeared. Ladders leaned against the walls. There was a screen for sifting adobe and sand and a long box to mix them in. A man drove up with a load of sand. Julio said the sand was no good, refused to accept it. The sand-seller retreated before a barrage of Spanish, and Julio called a *primo* who was an honorable man.

"My boy" sifted and mixed the adobe mortar. Julio, his red socks twinkling, ran up and down the ladder and finally perched like a gnome on the fire wall. "My boy" filled two big buckets with mud and started up the ladder. It collapsed beneath him and, for a moment it was hard to tell what was adobe and what was laborer.

"My father say," translated "my boy," wiping adobe from his face, "you have to start with the fire walls and work down."

"Of course," I agreed, "you have to have the fire walls strong, so the pine tree ceiling beams will not catch fire."

On interpretation of my remark, Julio fairly screamed, "Not for fire-engine fire. Fire walls from old days—bang, bang when *Los Indios* make war." He loaded an imaginary musket, crouched behind the fire wall and shot round after round into a seething mass of Apaches and Comanches. The dramatics were still going on as I retreated into the house.

Soon a deep-set window was discovered that would not open nor shut, due to a slight sag in the wall. "I have boy named Cipriano," offered Julio. "He is carpenter." Later Cipriano came by and was formally presented with much hand-shaking and kind inquiries. Unfortunately, Cipriano was on crutches, due to a recent misadventure. "He boss job," Julio arranged. " 'Nother boy, named Solomón, do the work."

Solomón was produced from around the corner and was likewise formally presented. The place simply swarmed with "my boys." Repair work went on apace. Julio moulded and smoothed. When he came to the north side of the building, he descended the ladder and almost wept. "Beeg 'oles," he moaned, wringing his adobe crusted hands, "beeg as *cavernas.*"

Solomón discovered an electrical fixture that did not operate. Happily he instigated repairs. But evidently he was not an electrician, because every fuse in the house exploded with a loud report that recalled the recent Apache raid, and I almost took to the shelter of the fire walls. My refrigerator, my furnace thermostat, my radio, my clock, and every light in the house went out. The Public Service Company responded to an emergency call.

But, by Saturday morning, the Little Adobe House was its pristine self again with all its hand-gentled corners and rosy color. Happily I wrote checks for Julio and all his "boys." A half hour before bank closing time, Julio returned. "Bank no cash checks," he confided. "Maybe you no got money enough."

Then I remembered that, months ago, due to a lost checkbook, with my easily copied handwriting on the stubs, the bank had alerted its cashiers to scrutinize any checks with my signature against possible forgery. Evidently checks made out Julio, Ambrosio, Cipriano, and Solomón Melendez had alerted the bank employees like a burglar alarm. It was only through the efforts of the president of the bank that I could persuade them to give the "all quiet" signal. As it was almost closing time and Julio and his "boys" said they must have cash for week-end expenditures, there was nothing for it but to call a taxi and send them rolling elegantly bankward.

How quiet and peaceful was the Little Adobe House!

The Stillness Here

THE LITTLE
Adobe House is a mile and a quarter from
the plaza, on a dirt road which ends abruptly
at the foot of hills rolling like waves up
toward the Butterfly Mountains. I am glad
that the little house is on a dead-end, rutty
street. There is stillness.

"How quiet it is," city dwellers sigh
as they look out on pear blossoms tapping
against brown walls, or on green treetops
moving languidly in the breeze, or golden
autumn leaves floating indolently by. Few
of the visitors know the vast stillness that
enfolds the little house in winter.

Just let four or five inches of high-alti-
tude, powdery snow blanket the yard, outline
portal walls, and press a dunce cap of white
whimsy on flat roofs, and I take up residence
in an amazing world. I look out of deep-set windows, much as a person in a diving bell must

look out on recognizable but strange undersea life.

The school children, who go through the yard twice a day, are oddly distorted. One extremity is clumsy with boots or galoshes, the other is ballooned out of all proportion with mufflers and ear tabs. Old ladies wrap their faces in black shawls until only a circle of eye shows. All pass silently as ghosts and I wonder if they are real.

My neighbor's big, white St. Bernard dog looks like a polar bear in their snow-filled yard. When Mr. Apodaca leads out his goats to nibble the frozen tips of bushes along the snowy hillside, I wave to them not as well-known neighbors, but as I might salute some fragment of Grecian bas-relief.

Within the thick walls of the little house, the stillness is not that of a vacuum, but a stillness that points up delicate sounds seldom noted. Piñon logs in the corner fireplace burn with a shy whispering. They do not crackle and snap like other wood. That diffident whisper is the same sound I have heard out in the piñon forests when they thought no one was listening.

Because of that whispering, I revisit all the forests I have ever known—the untouched wilderness along the Yukon, where caribou come down to drink; forests strung with blue glacial lakes in the Canadian Rockies; mist-hazed forests in Mexico, where Tarascan women in red petticoats gather firewood; cataract-sprayed yellow pines in the Yosemite back country. Whenever I have been in a forest, my first thought has always been: How I would love to see it in winter! Bewitched by the whispering piñon fire, I can see those forests vividly as they must be in winter, the illimitable whiteness, the blue and lavender shadows, even the beguiling footprints of little animals.

Another gentle sound becomes audible when snow begins to melt in wooden roof-gutters. At first it is a slow drip, drip, but by noon it becomes an elfin tinkle. With that sound, I hear the soft tinkle of tiny, snow-water streams in alpine meadows, where pink-tipped daisies bloom. I hear the first tinkle of ice-released water down our little "deetches." I know that, at that sound, men in a dozen Spanish villages back in the mountains will be getting out their battered hoes and shovels. I saw such a man in

Cundiyó turning over the moist soil along a little stream. As he shoveled, he would bring up pieces of broken pottery with almost every shovelful. He shook his head. "Every year it is the same—the broken pots of the ancients in my garden plot."

Those minute sounds in the winter-muffled house are due more to an awareness than to hearing. Late in the autumn there was much talk about a comet that was to be seen in the dawn sky. I paid little attention to the frantic setting of alarm clocks and the reported spot in the sky where the wonder was supposed to be seen.

Contrary to custom, early in the morning, I was suddenly awake, quite sure that something momentous was happening. I ran to a window and there, over the flat roof of a wing of the house, was a great light. It was so big and bright, at first I thought it must be a forest fire in the Butterfly Mountains. But it was the planet Venus, low in the early winter dawn sky. It looked half as big as a full moon. Then a lesser light moved rapidly by the planet. At first I thought it was a falling plane, but then I knew it was the much-talked-about comet.

I was one of the few people in Santa Fé who saw that glorious sight. Without benefit of alarm clocks I saw Venus in her accustomed place in the orderly heavens. I saw the comet moving in its wild course headlong on its wanderings.

Hugh Judge said: "How good it is to retire into quietness! As food is to the body, so is quietude to the mind."

Cousin Canuto
and the Assembly Line

THE MOST beguiling shops in Santa Fé are not the curio stores, dear to *turistas*. Rather are they the *tiendacitas* of the natives. You find them scattered about in strange, out-of-the-way places—along the little water "deetches," tucked into unknown *placitas,* and hidden in adobe homes.

Such a store is Cousin Canuto's. Like all the others, it is one room of his adobe home. To go into it to buy is to become a member of the family. You become involved with the family washing, the latest baby, and visiting relatives as far away as Trampas. You also discover the financial situation of the patrons.

All winter long the credit slips on the nails behind the counter grow thicker and thicker. Day laborers find little work during the snowy months. But by mid-summer you can see at a glance that the Archuletas have reduced their debt by half and the Vigils by only a third, due to the new baby. Usually, by autumn most of the credit nails are clear. Alas, with the first snowfall, the little slips of paper begin to pile up again in exact ratio to the snow.

In spite of the discouraging evidence, Cousin Canuto clung to his little store. Time and again, the serve-self market in which he had once worked as a checker at the fabulous salary of two hundred a month, asked him to return. Being a hopeless romantic, he had exchanged an adequate income for nails full of credit slips and a chance to sing around the old wood stove on winter days and on the hollyhock-shadowed doorstep when the sun was shining.

It was, therefore, surprising to see him passing through my yard regularly mornings and nights. Evidently, he had returned to regular employment and a regular pay check. He might be working for wages, but his passage had the air of a man propelled on the wings of a cause. I wondered what rosy cloud of romance wrapped this deflection from Cousin Canuto's ideas of the good life.

One morning when he was a little early,

he stopped to explain. *"Sí Señora,* my oldest *muchacho,* Tomasito, is running the little store with the help of his mother. It is time he learns something of business methods." Then with shining eyes and many gestures, he told me of the cause.

"Some day," he grieved, "there may be no adobe *casitas* in Santa Fé. You know how they are building now—with pumice blocks and hollow tile and cement. Some day, Señora, an adobe house will become as rare as a hand-carved *santo.* The *ricos* will buy them all up and you and I will be living in houses you hear about over the radio—houses all cut and measured, with the exact number of nails done up in little packages. *Ay,* we will have no houses that grow with the years and our living, but houses stamped out of men's money-making minds like pieces of lifeless metal. *¡Ay!"*

Cousin Canuto's face brightened. "But things are not as dark as they seem, Señora. A man here is making adobe bricks by what you Anglos call assembly line ways. You know how hard it has always been to find good adobe bricks when you wanted to build. If you did not make your own, you had to pick them up,

151

a few here and a few there in people's yards. Now this assembly yard man is making them by the thousands. You can pick up your *teléfono* and order as many as you need. Inside of an hour, a truck will dash up to your yard and deliver your order. I felt, Señora, I must help in my poor way, so fine a cause. There must be more adobe houses in Santa Fé."

He strode off as one who wears a crusader's coat of mail and carries a shining sword. Only as an afterthought, he remarked that the wholesale grocery men did not seem to understand the long winter months when men had no work and the credit slips piled up on the nails.

As the summer went by, Cousin Canuto lost the air of a crusader. He dragged through my yard at nightfall as wearily as any other begrimed worker. Gone was the knight in shining armor. Gone was the song that signaled his passing.

I found him shortly thereafter behind the counter of his little store. "Ah, Señora," he beamed, "the wholesale grocery men are paid." What was another winter to Cousin Canuto?

"Confidentially," he whispered, "that adobe bricks by the assembly line was a great disappointment. I soon saw that it was not in their nature to be that way. Ten trucks hauling in adobe *tierra* from all over the country, blue from out Tesuque way, red from Pecos, brown from the hills back of Santa Fé! What color could you get with such a mixture? Twenty men sifting, twenty men mixing, twenty filling the forms, twenty stacking the bricks. Something terrible gets into handmade things when too many are made at once, Señora. My *esposa* says it is true even of too many *frijoles* cooking in a kettle."

"But the *muchacho,* Tomasito, he was to learn business methods in the store?"

"He has found his own business, Señora. He is now in the newspaper business—as delivery boy. He had to have a bicycle and I now pay ten dollars a month on it to give him a start."

"But it will soon be winter again and the credit slips will cover the nails behind your counter as the snow covers the ground."

"But it is still warm," Cousin Canuto insisted earnestly. "Saturday night I give a dance in the store to celebrate my escape from the assembly line. Be sure to come, Señora."

Return
of Private Padilla

IT WAS
during the war that Mrs. Apodaca took me up
to see her native village, in the blue shadow of
Truchas Peak. "The son of my *prima* has
returned on furlough from the Army of the
U Esse. Tomorrow we go in the truck from
the woodyard of Mrs. Pomposo Archuleta.
Maybe you like to go along? No? We go to welcome Private Padilla."

There was a certain air of the fanfare of
trumpets in the way she rolled the words, Private Padilla, on her tongue. If he had been a
four-star general, she could not have rolled
them with greater unction.

I remembered when Private Padilla had
left for training-camp. I had happened to see
him walking up and down San Francisco Street,
in Santa Fé, as he waited for the bus. He was a

154

boy from one of the little adobe villages in the mountains, where the customs of medieval Spain still live on in an American state. His faded blue Levis were tucked into high-heeled cowman's boots that gave him an amusing mincing gait. His shirt was the brightest cerise. Under his battered felt hat, black hair grew down about his ears in narrow triangles.

Out of a brown, impassive face, round eyes looked curiously at the mild metropolitan sights of Santa Fé. One hand held a bundle tied up in a cowman's bright neckerchief. Under the other arm, a battered guitar was pressed tight against the cerise shirt. I remembered a catch in my throat as I looked at a boy starting for mechanized war with a guitar under his arm.

The village of Private Padilla clings like a groundbird's nest to sun-glazed, tawny hills. Back of it, in painted steps, mountains rise to snow-topped summits. In front, through a pink arroyo, an irresponsible stream chuckles toward the Rio Grande. In that village there is no store, no post office, no telephone. Electric wires have never reached it. Incredibly the speech that the old ones use there is the Spanish of Cervantes.

Private Padilla's mother had hastened her spring cleaning in honor of his return. The door to the little, thick-walled house was fresh with paint the color of the piñon jay. "Blue," Mrs. Apodaca nodded, "the color of Mary, Queen of Heaven. No evil can get into a house with a blue door."

Inside, the walls had been freshly white-washed and polished with a piece of sheepskin. A long table, covered with gay oilcloth, held the center of the room. Around it beds ranged up and down, placed end to end. From a big, black cook-stove came enticing odors of meat balls bouncing about in a sauce *muy, muy, picante.*

When the good, peppery food had been passed and re-passed, we all walked out to look at the garden plot in a level hollow between the hills. Private Padilla asked many questions. How had the goats been? And the sheep? And the chickens? Had there been plenty of beans and corn and squash from the garden last year?

His *papá* hesitated. The rains had not come at the right times last summer. Lupita, who was now the goat boy, had to lead her charges far over the hills. And as for the garden—they carried all the water from the stream in the pink arroyo, bucket by bucket, in the dryest months. They had managed to get half a crop and then the stream had dried up. But that was nothing new.

One by one, the rest of the company left, until only Private Padilla and I were walking through the chamisa bushes. Under a gray-limbed cottonwood tree, a burro was tied, still in his winter overcoat of matted hair. His ridiculous long ears pointed to attention at the sound of voices.

"It is Pícaro," Private Padilla said. "Pícaro brings down the winter wood from the mountains for us on his back. When planting time comes, we hitch him to that little plow over there and *papá* scratches the garden plot."

I glanced at the little plow. It was hardly more than a forked stick. Beside it leaned feeble hoes and rusty crooked shovels. That was all the farming equipment there was on the place.

Private Padilla stood looking at the fragile farming implements. Suddenly he laughed and it was not pleasant laughter to hear. "There is a man in our unit," he said. "He is smart. He knows all about rocks and soil and water. He says that three—four hundred feet down in this part of the country is water that will never go dry. All we need is a well-digger's outfit. And then a little electric pump to raise the water."

Private Padilla's eyes ranged off across the color-filled mesaland. He laughed again, that unpleasant laughter. "And the nearest electric power line is forty miles away."

A Deal in Real Estate

the signs I have learned to recognize, Mrs.
Apodaca was upset. No old Spanish songs issued
from the weaving-room, in tune with the flying shuttle. With unusual haste she was
whitewashing a room vacated by Miguelito
and Mary-Ho when they moved into the hybrid
casita.

Whatever the disturbance was, it soon
spread to Cousin Canuto's *placita*. He spent
no time strumming his guitar in the radiated
warmth of warm adobe walls. He was busily
engaged in counting adobe bricks and marking
off what seemed to be the foundation for a
new room.

I have learned to ask no questions of my
neighbors and have thereby acquired a vast
patience in this land which is one great question

159

mark. But the unusual tensions that possessed Mrs. Apodaca and Cousin Canuto spread rapidly through Tenorio Flat. Men stood grouped together after work and talked in low tones. Women huddled together and nodded their thoughtful heads.

This was perplexing enough, but soon people from distant villages began arriving in slow-moving wood-wagons. How could they leave their chile-stringing and their blue-corn-drying to come to Santa Fé? How could they leave their flocks of sheep, so lately driven down from mountain meadows? Nothing seemed to happen, after prolonged conferences. They climbed into homeward-bound wagons as glumly as they had left them hours before.

Cousin Canuto progressed from counting bricks to laying them in thick walls for an adobe room. "It will be a room, *magnifico,*" he pointed out, hurling adobe mortar about like a human volcano. "Windows on the east and south for the sun, and there will be a corner fireplace for the piñon logs. *Mi abuelo* [grand-father], the old one, will like it."

So that was it! Cousin Canuto lowered his voice. "An Anglo *pintor,* a man who paints pictures, has offered the old one four thousand dollars for his old house and a few acres in the village. The *pintor* is leaving the world and all its works in disgust. All he wants to do is to paint pictures. It is a great price to pay. *Mi abuelo* will be a rich man, Señora. But he will need a home. It is natural that I, his only close relative in the state, should provide it. And it will not cost him one cent. You cannot buy a home."

Next day Mrs. Apodaca, who was only a *prima* of the old one, showed me the room she had prepared. It was freshly whitewashed, and red curtains hung at the little windows. "The old one will like this room," Mrs. Apodaca declared. After all, Cousin Canuto has many *muchachos* and the turmoil of his store. Better the peace and quiet I can give him. And it will not cost him one penny. It will be an honor to have the old one with me. Perhaps he can help Carmencita with the contests."

In turn, Mrs. Archuleta and Mrs. Vigil showed me the rooms they had prepared. Although they were *primas* further removed than Mrs. Apodaca, they felt their adobes were better adapted as homes for the old one.

One brisk October day, Cousin Canuto borrowed a gasping car and took me to see the object of the great real estate deal. Unfortunately, the old one had departed for the mountains on a piñon-picking expedition, but Patrocina Pacheco, a neighbor, was there.

Truly, any *pintor* in words or paints would gladly leave the world for such a place. The house was very old, with walls three feet thick. Windows looked off across a shining valley to the blue frigate of Jemez Mountain. A stream dropped down from snowy heights to water minute fields and an orchard of gnarled apple and apricot trees.

"Since the old one was left alone, I have looked out for him," said Patrocina Pacheco. "Now that he is selling his house, it is better that he move in with my family. It is bad to uproot one so old. Better stay in the village where he has always lived," and she cast a withering glance at Cousin Canuto.

Two days after we returned from the village, Cousin Canuto stopped work on the new room. Just as suddenly, Carmencita took over the renovated room in her mother's *casita*. The Señoras Archuleta and Vigil, rented their rooms to utter strangers. The *pintor* was observed in the ticket office disconsolately buying transportation to parts unknown.

The next time I went up to Cousin Canuto's store, I discarded all standards of courtesy and asked a question. "What has become of the old one?"

Cousin Canuto sighed, but there was a twinkle in his eyes and pride in his voice. *"Helas,* Señora, *mi abuelo* is not moving to Santa Fé. He is not moving anywhere. He is not selling his house to the *pintor* or to anyone. In spite of four thousand dollars his house is not for sale. It never has been. It was the *pintor* who did all the talking. *Mi abuelo* never said he would sell. How people like the *pintor* jump to conclusions!"

The Line
of Mrs. Apodaca's Hem

BETWEEN
Christmas and Twelfth Night, Mrs. Apodaca
went about with shining eyes and a carefully
controlled smile. She was the picture of a
woman who knows a delicious secret which she
is keeping strictly to herself.

But Armendita showed no shining eyes
nor smiling lips. There was to be a Twelfth
Night *baile* in Cousin Canuto's little store.
Tenorio Flat was planning to attend to a man
and Armendita's swain was driving in the long,
snowy miles from Chimayó.

Armendita brought her worried young
face and her exasperations to the calm shelter
of the Little Adobe House. Over her arm she
carried her best dress of peach-colored rayon.
"It's the prettiest dress I have," she lamented,
"but look where it comes on me."

The pinkish-yellow rayon covered her knees by only an inch or two. It was as dated as last year's blue jay's nest.

"I tried to get some of that bias hem-facing material," she sighed, "but there isn't an inch left in Santa Fé."

From the strange appearance of some of the hem lines about town, I was not surprised. Then I remembered a bolt I had on hand when I definitely relinquished all efforts toward the "new look." "Here's some," I offered, "even if it is turquoise blue. Sew it in carefully and it won't show. Then send the dress to the cleaner—and there you are." I should have known better!

In a few days, Armendita was back with the peach-colored rayon. It was longer now by a good three inches, but the line of former stitching stood out like a whipcord and fairly shrieked, "Let down, let down." We got out the ironing-board and iron. We steamed that hem line and pressed it on the wrong side. Still it screamed "Let down." We pressed it with much vigor on the right side under a fold of white cloth. We rubbed it gently with the fingertip and not so gently with the fingernail,

165

as all the women's magazines advised. It did not do a bit of good.

"Never mind," I tried to comfort. "There will be many like it at the party and Cousin Canuto's store will not be brightly lighted. Wear your new silver slippers and no one will look at your hem line."

"Sometimes," wept Armendita, "I wish I wore long black skirts to my ankles like *mamacita*—year in and year out. She doesn't have to worry when fashions change."

Twelfth Night is the peak of all holiday festivities in Spanish-American homes, I remembered, as I felt my way along the frozen water-ditch on the night of Cousin Canuto's party. In remote villages, children would be putting out their shoes filled with straw for the camels of the Three Kings. In Santa Fé, from Agua Fria Street to Atalaya Hill, adobe walls would expand to take in all who came. The hum of guitars and the pat of dancing feet would make gay many a snowy *placita*.

Cousin Canuto's store had been garnished for the occasion. Like a lighthouse in the center of the room, the fat, iron stove glowed red with heat from piñon wood. Overhead were streamers of pink and blue crepe paper. I felt a warmth in my heart for a people who would see only pink and blue streamers, and not grocery shelves scantily stocked with cans of tomatoes and washing powder.

Along the sides of the room, like an inked-in frieze, sat the women of Mrs. Apodaca's generation. Their dresses, with full black skirts, merged with the shadows. Only the twinkling of a gold earring showed that portion of the room to be inhabited. Babies slept peacefully in the midst of twanging guitars and scraping fiddles. The center of the floor was packed with dancing young people who were flitting about in the modern steps to which they gave a decided Latin rhythm and joy.

As they danced, they sang. Here a voice lifted alone; others joined in until the strings of drying onions and *ristras* of chile dangling from the ceiling beams fairly swayed with the impetus.

"Ah," greeted Cousin Canuto, tucking his guitar under his arm, "a cold, snowy night it is for camels of the desert to be going about our country. But a star to follow gives warmth to the heart. No, Señora?" And he joined in the chorus that was swelling through the room.

When the young people had danced and sung all they could and were refreshing themselves with bottles of pink and green soda pop, some of the older guests called for the old dances. Cousin Canuto led Mrs. Apodaca to the center of the floor. All chatter stopped as the black-clad woman and the man in blue overalls danced the old steps they knew and loved.

For awhile, they were so entranced with Mrs. Apodaca's shawl flying out behind her, her swaying gold earrings and floor-skimming feet that they did not notice anything startling in her appearance. Then a gasp whispered through the room. I could scarcely believe my own eyes. But it was true. Mrs. Apodaca's black full skirts were at least six inches shorter than they had ever been before. They were short enough to show her high-laced, black kid shoes and even a small portion of her decent, black cotton stockings.

Not One Auk

IT WAS
early in the winter that a table for the birds
seemed a charming and poetic idea. Conse-
quently, I contrived a somewhat wobbly affair
and placed it under a window in the sheltered
angle of warm adobe walls. But that turquoise-
blue table for New Mexico's winged inhabitants
has not had an exactly peaceful influence on
my quiet, adobe days.

It has upset my work, my orderly hours,
my relationship with Tenorio Flat, with
Koshare, my cat, and with dear friends at a
distance. Unfortunately, another window,
under which stands my typewriter table, looks
out on the bird caravansary. What are those
two brown birds with spotted waistcoats and
cross-barred tails? I consult the immense tome,
Birds of New Mexico, for at least two hours
before I discover that they are canyon wrens.

After that, the flight of words cannot compete with the flight of wings.

My supplies of bread and cereals are chronically depleted, now that I am running a bird hotel. At strange hours, I must dash up to Cousin Canuto's *tiendacita* to buy a few necessities for my own table. If the morning is cold, I am busy with pottery bowls of warm water. If snow has fallen during the night, the bird table must be brushed and fresh viands provided.

My feeling toward the blue-winged piñon jay has changed. Once I delighted in the flash of his sky-colored wings against brown walls. Now I am constantly on the alert to dash out with a broom, so that he will not frighten the smaller birds away and make off with all the tid-bits of suet. *Bandidos,* those piñon jays are, swooping down with wild battle crys from their skulking places behind fat little chimneys.

Everyone predicted unspeakable actions on the part of Koshare. Koshare has grown even more Spanish with the years, until he is quite the grandee, with his Philip the Second ruff, his black velvet mantle down the exact center of his back, and his decorations from the courts of Europe on his chest. Koshare has great dignity now that he has passed kittenhood. It was a delight to me to report to various Cassandras that Koshare stalked past the bird table with never a glance to the left nor the right.

Then, one day, he evidently decided that the birds were receiving too much admiration and attention around the Little Adobe House. Now, whenever he can manage it, he sits on the bird table, drawn up in full grandee hauteur. But he never lifts a paw. Many times a day I have to remove him from the bird table and his cold war, and carry him ignominiously into the house.

As soon as the bird table became popular, "that Carmencita" started bringing the *muchachos* to see it. She even delivered a kind of guide-book speech with each exhibition. By twos and threes and even by the half-dozen, she led big-eyed children to see the birds. She went far afield for spectators, even to Cousin Canuto's *placita* and the adobes on Agua Fria Street.

Soon my peaceful evenings by the corner fireplace were interrupted by hesitant rappings at the door. Embarrassed and harassed *papás* were being given no rest until they, too, constructed bird tables. Could they, *por favor,* measure mine? And "What did the *pajaritos* eat?"

I had visions of the whole bird population of New Mexico being coaxed into my immediate vicinity. I also had visions of *mamacitas* left breadless and suetless in adobe homes, where such commodities are not exactly overabundant.

After several weeks, "that Carmencita" came over one night, her pockets distended with dozens of sticks of bubble gum. "This is your share, Señora," she said, emptying handfuls into my lap. At my inquiry she gave me that wise, compasionate glance of hers and also an exultant laugh. It seems that every *muchacho* she had brought to see my bird guests had paid her an admission fee of one stick of bubble gum. She had, as it were, captured the concession on the bird table.

This was upsetting enough, but an erudite Anglo friend capped the climax. From her home down over La Bajada, she sent me a brief breathless plea. "Wire me when the first albatross shows up." As I did not deign to answer this, she followed with a sad monosyllabic message—"Not one auk yet?"

It would seem that the entertaining of birds should be a peaceful and poetic act. It has proved just as upsetting as Cousin Canuto's dramatic digressions.

Alas –
Poor Cousin Canuto!

COUSIN Canuto's Señora, María Lupita, seldom visits in Tenorio Flat. All the other neighborhood Señoras are great visitors. María Lupita not only has a large family, but she spends much time in the little store while her husband is occupied with more important affairs.

When she started passing through my yard almost daily, I began to wonder. From the shawl pulled tightly over her bowed head and drooping shoulders, I suspected that Cousin Canuto was off again on some dramatic tangent. She would stay a couple of hours in *Casita* Apodaca. Then she and Mrs. Apodaca would walk home together, their shawled heads both drooped disconsolately.

This passage of beshawled gloom went on for several weeks. At last Mrs. Apodaca wandered over to the Little Adobe House and sagged heavily into the big rocker before the corner fireplace. In spite of its friendly warmth, she wrapped her oldest shawl more tightly about her. *"Ay de mí*—alas—" she sighed, "María Lupita, *pobrecita,* poor little ones! Soon they will have no store. Soon they will have no roof over their heads." She wiped away a flood of tears with the end of her shawl. "Cousin Canuto will not pay his taxes. They are long overdue."

No matter how scarce money may be with my neighbors, taxes are usually paid. That is because they cherish their share of adobe *tierra* and the sturdy little homes they built with their own hands.

"Why, I saw Cousin Canuto pay his taxes last year," I gasped. "I was paying my own in the tax collector's office and there was Cousin Canuto. He took off his broad-brimmed hat and took out a handful of folded bills from under the sweat band."

"Always he has done that," Mrs. Apodaca sighed. "A dollar here and a dollar there, saved under the hat to pay the taxes on his *placita.* But not this year!"

"Is it," I inquired as delicately as possible, "that the credit slips in the store are piling up too high on the nails over the counter?"

"No, no," Mrs. Apodaca insisted, her eyes flashing. "Cousin Canuto has the money under his hat band now. He is mad at the government. Not all the government," she hastened to explain. "Just the part that runs our schools here. There was a piece in the paper. Maybe you saw it, Señora. It said they were going to teach the little ones in the lower grades a thing called natural science, which only the big *muchachos* have studied before. The piece says, so Cousin Canuto told me, that in this age of the atom, even the little ones should know what makes things blow up."

Mrs. Apodaca rocked and groaned. "Now he will not pay his taxes, he says, to keep such terrible schools going. He says he is going to take all his children out of school. They will grow up like little savages. For that, of course, Señora, he will be put in the *penitenciario*.

"Ay, Señora, it is a great tragedy. He wrote a letter to the Spanish newspaper, telling all the Spanish-American people to take their *muchachos* out of school. It took him a week to write that letter. It was many pages long and very beautiful. It sounded like singing—but not happy singing. You wanted to weep. *Ay de mi,* the Spanish newspaper printed only a line or two of that beautiful letter. Cousin Canuto told the newspaper man he would not take the paper any more.

"I think," confessed Mrs. Apodaca, "that it was my Carmencita who started Cousin Canuto on his terrible way. You know she takes our daily paper. She went up to see Cousin Canuto and asked him questions he could not answer—all about what is a thing called a gamma ray or a beta particle. Now he wants me to take her out of school."

"But you wouldn't do that," I urged. "Think of all Carmencita is learning in school."

"*Sí,*" nodded Mrs. Apodaca, forgetting her grief in pride. "*Sí,* do you know what she is going to learn next? She is saving her contest money to buy a brass horn. The school is going to show her how to play it and then she can march in the school band."

"*Ay de mi,*" I echoed and shuddered. It seemed to me that I would prefer a gamma ray or even a beta particle in the neighborhood if

Carmencita started to practice on that brass horn.

"Cousin Canuto went to the school board and pleaded with them not to teach the little ones what makes things blow up. But it did no good. Next September they start. So now Cousin Canuto will bring up a lot of *muchachos* with no learning and with no roof over their heads, because he will not pay his taxes."

At that she took her grief home. Gloom still surrounds *Casita* Apodaca like a black shawl. But María Lupita's children still frisk through my yard on their way to school. Wedges of cheese and cans of corn may still be bought in the little store. Its roof still keeps out the snows of winter. Cousin Canuto, with a red geranium in his hat band, stalks to and from the plaza like a Latin Hamlet. I can catch a few lines of the song he is singing. They are from an old song once popular in our Spanish-American villages.

"When I was in the *penitenciario*," sings Cousin Canuto, "unhappy was I."

The Little Man on the Plato

COUSIN Canuto's rôle of martyr has worn quite thin in the last few weeks. He still refuses to pay his taxes and threatens to take his children out of school if so much as a gamma ray or beta particle is mentioned in the class room. But it seems to me that he is clinging to his position only until he finds a dignity-preserving reason for discarding it.

When Santa Fé tried out its new traffic lights at the busiest corner across from the plaza, I shuddered to think what new fuel this costly innovation would bring to Cousin Canuto's smoldering flame. There would be, probably, a five-page letter to the estimable city council and a refusal to comply with local pedestrian traffic regulations.

As I stood with other bewildered citizens

watching the new traffic lights flash red, yellow, green, and blue, I saw Cousin Canuto leaning against their tall, orange standard. He was wrapped in indolence and gloom. He stood with the rest of us watching the police scold and encourage the bewildered traffic. It was a sad snarl. Santa Fé had never faced such a situation before.

As Cousin Canuto stood watching the flashing lights, his face suddenly beamed with his old-time smile. The mantle of the martyr disappeared as if by magic. *"Rojo,"* sang out Cousin Canuto calling the colors as they appeared, *"amarillo, verde, azul."* It made a tune. When the *azul* [blue] light flashed, he, too, flashed into action. *"¡Vamos!"* he shouted and stalked across the narrow street as if he were leading a caparisoned army. On the other side of the street he waited until *azul* light flashed again. *"¡Vamos!"* he shouted again and stalked back. He did this a half-dozen times.

Then the rhythm and flashing colors bewitched him. *"Rojo, amarillo, verde, azul,"* chanted Cousin Canuto, as he winged his way back and forth in perfect tempo. He guided befuddled old ladies. He carried babies and huge shopping bags. He shepherded giggling little girls. The traffic police had very little to do.

I learned later that a five-page letter in Spanish was written to the city council. "I asked," Cousin Canuto explained "if one of the fine new traffic signals could not be placed on the road that leads to my *placita*—seeing that I am a taxpayer and the *papá* of many school children."

The road that leads to Cousin Canuto's *placita* is dusty and filled with chuck-holes. It is dead-end. In the course of twenty-four hours, three or four cars may jolt down it. Otherwise, the traffic consists of a wagon or two headed for piñon wood in the mountains, a man on horseback, a boy on burroback, and innumerable dogs and the six goats of *placita* residents.

"They could not do it at this time," Cousin Canuto explained tolerantly. "There are, of course, many busier streets in Santa Fé. However, Señora, I plan to build my own traffic signal. It would not, naturally, be run by electricity, but I could have colored glass signals of some kind with little tin shutters to cover and uncover them. They could be opened and shut by means of small ropes by someone stationed there for the purpose. It would be good training for the school children."

"But the school children do not use that road," I protested. "They come down the trail by the water ditch and through my yard. It cuts off at least three-quarters of a mile for them."

"*Si*," agreed Cousin Canuto, "but I may have to insist that they go the long way around. In this Age of the Atom," remarked Cousin Canuto sententiously, "the *muchachos* must be trained to take care of themselves—both on the land and in the air."

To my great joy, he has not been able to work on his traffic signal. A far greater enterprise has developed. "Señora," he gasped two days later, "you have, no doubt heard about the little man on the *plato*."

"*Plato, plato,*" I puzzled—"the little man on the plate?"

My excited friend nodded and pulled from under his hat a worn clipping. "It happened down on our own White Sands. A man, an admiral in our navy, I think it was, saw several times a *plato* whirling through the air at a terrible speed. He thinks the *plato* was made on one of the stars and that the man running it was trying to see what kind of people live here.

"Without a doubt," whispered Cousin Canuto, "that man from another star wishes to land in New Mexico. Just as strange things have happened here, the old ones tell us. Our region is full of things no one can explain. Anything could happen here."

I nodded, speechless, and quite carried away.

"Señora, someone should welcome that brave little man when he makes a landing with his *plato*. It might even happen that he would land in my *placita*. Should he do so, I am at a loss how to address him. Naturally, I would say, '*bienvenido, Señor, mi casa es suya*—welcome, sir, my house is yours.' But probably he will not understand Spanish, nor English, nor Indian Tewa, which also I speak.

"But I have a plan for that, Señora. The old ones have told me that the Indians of every tribe and even your English-speaking explorers, in the old days, had a sign language everyone could understand. I will learn that sign language, Señora. I have borrowed the horse of my *primo*, Pantalones Padilla. I shall ride to all the Indian pueblos around here. Perhaps some old Indian there remembers the sign language. If not, I am off to the land of the the Navaho. Surely, some aged Navaho will remember how to say in sign language, *'Bienvenido, Señor, mi casa es suya.'* "

Gadgets Invade Tenorio Flat

THE SUMMER evening lingered in my garden, like a pool of still water among the shadows. Nearby mountains showed splotches of rust and mulberry blue through a luminous veil of pine forests. A calliope hummingbird zoomed through the branches of the wild plum tree. From Tenorio Flat came the sleepy voices of children and the tranquil whisper of water in the little "deetch."

Suddenly, the artist's keen eyes noticed a raw upturning of soil along the edge of my adobe lot. "What have you been digging there?" he asked lazily.

From that moment, tranquility departed from the peaceful atmosphere of the little garden. Even the orange day-lilies and the blue delphinium merged discreetly with the shadows against the Little Adobe House.

"It is a trench for a gas pipe," I said strangely embarrassed. "I signed an impressive legal document, granting the Gas Company permission to run their line there. You see, Mrs. Apodaca has bought a gas range."

If I had announced that Mrs. Apodaca had bought a gilded elephant, my friends could not have been more greatly shocked.

After a painful silence, the poet cast his cowboy hat on the ground in a gesture of dismay. "I knew it would come," he wailed. "The era of gadgets is upon us. Even Tenorio Flat is not safe. Mrs. Apodaca with a gas range!"

"We might as well kiss it all good-by," the artist snorted. "A few more years and there won't be any beauty or its essence, simplicity, on the face of the earth. This was one of its last havens. And now—Mrs. Apodaca with a gas range!"

I sat remembering Mrs. Apodaca's kitchen, as I had known it on bleak snowy mornings when the big, iron cook-stove purred with piñon wood. I remembered the delicious aroma of drying chiles and blue corn which festooned the whitewashed walls. I thought wistfully of Mrs. Apodaca, as she moved gently, among her bubbling saucepans and her geraniums. I could not picture her tending a gas flame or setting an oven-heat indicator.

And then I remembered hot, summer, noondays when Mrs. Apodaca's weary face bent over the same steaming saucepans, as she cooked for her big family. "Did you every try cooking a meal for a big family on an August day?" I asked. "I'm glad Mrs. Apodaca is going to have a gas range. I hope every woman in Tenorio Flat will have a gas range!"

The artist jumped to his feet and paced wrathfully up and down among the hollyhocks. "I tell you what I am going to do," he declared. "I'm going to start painting as I've never painted before. I've got to get it all on canvas—the little golden houses, with their silver plumes of piñon smoke, the grace of shawl-wrapped heads—before it is gone."

"You'd better," I chuckled. "Soon, I hope, there will be a string of high-powered electric wires to every remote adobe village. And electric refrigerators and pressure water. And hard surfaced roads and . . ."

"Tourist cars roaring up and down them and 'Shady Nook' auto courts under every cottonwood tree," the artist interrupted. "And radios screaming from every mesa top, and hot-dog stands in our cedar forests!" He pointed a long finger at the poet. "And you—someone should lock you up until you catch in words the beauty that is on its way out."

But the poet did not seem to hear. He sat with his eyes fastened on the dim tops of blue and silver mountains.

"Beauty can't vanish," I said for him. "It is not ephemeral. It is the most hardy and persistent manifestation in the universe. Look at Mrs. Apodaca and her race. They can take mud from the ground and make the most charming of homes, which you and I copy rather poorly. Look at their blue-hooded wells and their wattled fences and their singing water ditches. Their sense of beauty is not plastered on the outside, nor gleaned from books. It wells up from inside. It has persisted in poverty and isolation. I am not in the least alarmed."

Mrs. Apodaca was moving softly about in her blue-shadowed garden. From it came the fragrance of the chamisa bush and the scent of water on sun-baked adobe.

Mrs. Apodaca's Compass

IN THESE days of early summer, I like to stand in my adobe yard and turn my thoughts to the four points of the compass. With gardening tools spread indolently about me, I make a great circle of the region I love, without moving a foot.

Much wandering through the years in all directions has impressed regional pictures so deeply on my heart that places a hundred miles away are as vivid as my wild plum tree, now spangled with jade-green fruit.

Up to the north, in Taos Canyon, the blue and white violets will be blooming along a mountain stream. All over the damp meadow lands, wild iris will be repeating the color tones of blue and purple mountains and bluer atmosphere. In the villages in the shadow of Truchas Peak, serious-faced men will be guiding small streams of water to chile and corn patches. Women will have their lambs' wool mattresses and pillows out in the sun. With slender rods, they will be stirring and beating the fluffy mass while the smoke from their outdoor ovens fills the air with cedar aroma.

In Chimayó, the cherries will be ripening, red against brown walls. All the village weavers will be starting newer, brighter blankets in their big looms. Across the mesa tops, shepherds will be leading their flocks to high mountain meadows.

To the south, along the Rio Grande, the sun will be hotter and the season more advanced. Corn, planted after intricate rites of dancing and chanting, will be growing lustily in fields around the Indian pueblos. Potters sit in warm, adobe dooryards and build, coil on coil, their graceful jars and bowls. On every windblown hilltop from Acoma to Santo Domingo, along the highway, Indian women sit with their wares about them under wattled shelters.

Eastward, my mind follows deep canyons, wooded with elfin forests of piñon and cedar. In their midst stands Pecos ruin, soft red against the sky. I remember how I saw it one summer night under a full moon. It was a place not of this world, its outlines melting into immensity.

Beyond, where the elfin forests merge with dark towering yellow pines, I once started a herd of antelope. A high altitude hailstorm was pelting the earth with frozen pellets as big as marbles. The white-rumped animals jumped high in the air at each onslaught as if propelled on wires. Overhead, lightning made arrow etchings against the black sky.

Westward, the Hopis will be looking from their terraced mesas across the heat-swirling desert to blue-glass mountains. Men will trot ten miles to their small, spring-watered fields. At night, they will trot ten miles back to their high-perched homes under the desert stars.

Not far from them, the Navahos will be headed toward their thatched summer homes in the shelter of painted rocks. White-topped covered wagons will stir the red dust of an intricate spider web of dirt roads. Men, women, and children will race on horseback through sunny valleys and across mesa tops. A whole tribe will establish summer residence as gaily as migrating birds. The loom will go up between two twisted cedar trees. Children will guide the new lambs to water holes. Women will sit on cloud-flecked hilltops and watch both lambs and children. Truly, "The People" will be walking "The Beautiful Way" of which they sing.

During this vast circle of mental visitation to the four points of the New Mexican compass, my gardening tools had been idle. Dimly, all the time, I had been aware of unusual activity around *Casita* Apodaca. There is the sound of a rake hitting stones, of a hoe attacking weeds, of trash cans being emptied, of water being pulled from the well. Then there is a great silence. Suddenly Mrs. Apodaca stands before me. A flour sack replaces the shawl, always the symbol of intense activity.

"So long you stand here, Señora," Mrs. Apodaca rebukes.

I describe to her the mental journey I have just made. I tell her I have boxed the compass in its cardinal points, North, East, South, and West, without so much as moving a foot.

"Ah," agrees Mrs. Apodaca. "Did you

know, Señora, that *los Indios,* who are wise about such things, have two more directions? Not only do they have North, East, South, and West, but they have Up and Down."

A twinkle flared in her eyes beneath the flour sack. "And I, Señora, have still another one. It is *El Centro*—the center. It is good, Señora, to know in what direction you go, whether it is East, West, South, or North, or Up or Down. But it is *muy, muy importante* to know where you stand right now. That is *El Centro.*"

Grace Is a Flowering

FAUSTIN
is Mrs. Apodaca's grandson, being the son of Miguelito and Mary-Ho. Frost was scarcely out of the ground, before he started his big project. The lot of his *papá* is a long, narrow one. Across the two-hundred-foot frontage, Faustín had marked out almost a straight line with wobbly sticks and much-knotted cord. Guided by the cord, he was laboriously digging a deep trench. His back bent over the heavy pick and curved under the long shovel handle.

Week after week the trench grew deeper and longer. Late spring snows whitened Faustín's bony shoulders and reddened his hands. From school-close to darkness, he labored on.

I could not ask him why he was digging the long trench. To do so would have branded me as a barbarian, one who did not understand the finer nuances of life. All I could do was to guess the reason for the long ditch in front of the house.

Shamefaced, I guessed another *casita* in Tenorio Flat was about to install a gas range. To save expenses, I reasoned, small Faustín was digging the trench for the connecting gas pipe. I thought how useless, for half a year, Mrs. Apodaca's stove had proved to be. Only during the hottest months does she use it. In winter, the iron cook-stove comes back into the picture. Then the gas range stands in her kitchen, white and gleaming, its top decorated with a vase containing paper roses. Its oven door is used as a background for a saint's picture glued to its surface.

After a month of day-by-day labor, Faustín's trench bounded the front of the lot—almost straight and a foot deep. But no truck from the Gas Company appeared to make the necessary connections. The ditch yawned, empty and unused—a trap for the belated foot traveler on dark nights and a question-mark to the curious.

At last the mystery was solved. Side by side like little soldiers, small whips of lilac bushes had been planted. Some day the *casita* of his *papá* will peer out on nodding purple plumes and their fragrance will drift through little windows to mingle with the good peppery scent of drying chiles.

That painful, persistent effort of a small boy—not for a gas pipe, but for a row of "lee-lacs"—is typical of the sense of values that flowers in daily grace among his people.

Even the occasional depredations of small neighbors have a grace all their own. When Little John Biscuit and fat little Dado raid my own lilac bushes and fill their arms with stolen blossoms, my Anglo friends protest shrilly, "Those children are stealing your flowers." But I know from much experience that the raiders of my lilac hedge will soon be tapping at my door. With shy, but elegant, courtesy, they will present me with nosegays filched from my own bushes.

Grace can even glorify a vendor of news-papers. Tomasito now sells papers on San Francisco Street as papers were never sold before. Instead of bundling them under his arm and assaulting the faces of buyers with a sample, Tomasito carries his whole pack doubled over his extended arms in front of him, much as a *toreador* waves a provocative cape. He swings down San Francisco Street with the air of a great actor treading a stage created for him alone.

When the Gutierrez family deserted their decrepit adobe in Tenorio Flat and moved back to Mora, they left, in one window, a geranium growing in an old lard can. As summer came along and the sun beat on the windows, the geranium shriveled and dried for want of water and care. Day-by-day it looked worse. I even made a search of the neighborhood to see if a key to the deserted house had been left, so that I could rescue the gallant little plant. But no one knew of a key. There was no way to get into the house.

One very hot day I found Mrs. Apodaca on her knees by the blue-covered well. She was packing good, oozing adobe soil into a big coffee can. As tenderly as she would straighten the limbs of a sleeping baby, she spread the parched roots of a drying geranium in moist, roomy soil. "It is the plant from the window of the Gutierrez house," she said. *"Pobrecita—* poor little thing—it did so want to live."

"But however did you get the window open?" I marveled.

Mrs. Apodaca gave the sweet inscrutable smile of an innocent angel and replied vaguely: "Someone threw a rock, a very little rock and broke the window under the little catch." As she sprinkled water over dry leaves, she remarked firmly, "Better a little piece of glass gets broken than a flower die."

Now, as I pass Mrs. Apodaca's window, I see that the Gutierrez geranium is waving a new bloom like a banner of victory. It is the biggest and reddest in the window. In a way, it has come to represent to me Mrs. Apodaca and her race, who have flowered in an arid land because their roots are good.